Getting it Right

Getting it Right
Making Corporate–Community Relations Work

Luc Zandvliet and Mary B. Anderson

Greenleaf
PUBLISHING

Published by
Greenleaf Publishing Limited
Aizlewood's Mill
Nursery Street
Sheffield S3 8GG
UK
www.greenleaf-publishing.com

Cover by LaliAbril.com.

Printed in Great Britain on acid-free paper by CPI Antony Rowe, Chippenham, Wiltshire.

FSC
Mixed Sources
Product group from well-managed
forests and other controlled sources

Cert no. SGS-COC-2953
www.fsc.org
© 1996 Forest Stewardship Council

British Library Cataloguing in Publication Data:
    A catalogue record for this book is available from the British Library.

    ISBN-13: 9781906093198

Contents

Figures and tables

Boxes

Preface and acknowledgments

Throughout this book, the authors relate vignettes about company–community relations. These stories are not fiction. They all report on real experiences of real people in real countries with real companies. However, in most places the authors report these stories in generalized terms, citing neither company nor country by name. There are two reasons for this.

First, the vignettes we selected are not about unique or bizarre situations. They represent experiences that we have seen in many places with many companies. They are chosen precisely because they highlight common and widely shared experiences that are important for learning how to improve company–community relations. To emphasize that the stories are broadly relevant across multiple contexts, we have not particularized either the country or the company.

Second, the purpose of this book is not to vilify or embarrass any company or community. Instead, the purpose of these stories and the lessons that they support is to build on broad experience in order to figure out how to do better in the future. Naming companies or countries where things go wrong would send the wrong message, implying that some companies get it wrong while others get it right. In our experience, most companies both get it wrong *and* get it right and the challenge is to figure out how to avoid the former and be consistent with the latter. These stories are meant to support this purpose.

CDA Collaborative Learning Projects, which is the organizational home of the Corporate Engagement Project (CEP), is institutionally committed to working with a broad range of international actors on many fronts, clearly judging the outcomes and impacts of the work of these actors but never condemning or condoning the individuals who act. The world is interconnected in many ways, and we believe that it is a better place when people cross borders, interact respectfully with other cultures, and appreciate the diversity of histories and mores that exist across this globe. It is a better place when people who have skills and abilities can apply these in settings where they can help improve the lives of local people. With these beliefs, we have worked for many years with individuals and agencies involved in humanitarian assistance, development cooperation, and conflict prevention and peace building.

When CDA undertook the work of the CEP in 2000, we recognized that alongside these assistance-focused groups a large number of commercial enterprises also affect the lives of people who live in poor or troubled societies. It seemed plausible and worthwhile to investigate these corporate impacts more closely in order to learn how these entities — which will continue to cross borders for work in the increasingly interconnected world — can ensure that they have positive, rather than negative, impacts on the lives and societies of local people.

CDA's approach in such investigations is what we call "collaborative learning." Our projects organize processes through which many actors (humanitarians, peace people, corporations) can gather and compare their field-based experience and, from this, identify patterns that are common across contexts. Analysis of these patterns, over time, allows us collaboratively to discern lessons about how to improve positive impacts and reduce negative impacts. The CEP has been organized in this same way. Many companies were invited to participate in a joint effort to assemble broad, practical field experience (through site-visit studies) and to work together to analyze it. A number of companies welcomed this approach and joined the project, submitting their field operations to intense visits by CEP teams who interviewed a broad range and number of people in those contexts about a company's operations and impacts. All site-visit reports are available on CDA's website (www.cdainc.com). In addition, several companies invited CEP representatives to internal workshops with their corporate social responsibility (CSR) practitioners to test the project findings against their own experiences, and many other companies participated in the CEP project through periodic consultations that we organized to review field findings.

From this background, it will be clear to readers that many people have been involved in the collection of experience and the range of ideas and approaches that have contributed to the learning in this book. Village people in many places, local religious leaders, business people, politicians, academics, security personnel, army commanders, rebel leaders, ambassadors and other embassy staff, corporate executives in headquarters and site managers in the field, and workers have all been willing to spend time with CEP teams, discussing and reflecting on how a company's activities have affected the lives of local people and the countries in which they have operations. These individuals are far too numerous to name and many prefer to remain anonymous in any case.

Nonetheless, it is important to acknowledge and thank the specific corporations whose staff have participated in field studies, in consultations, and in reflections on this material. The following companies have done this: AngloGold Ashanti, Antamina Mine, Anvil Mining, Barrick Gold Corporation, BG Group, BHP Billiton, BP, ChevronTexaco, ConocoPhillips, Eni Group, Exxon Mobil Corporation, F&C Investments, Greystar Resources, Newmont Mining Corporation, Placer Dome (now part of Barrick), Premier Oil, Shell, Talisman Energy, Total, and Unocal.

It is also useful to list the countries where intensive site visits occurred to give the readers some indication of the range and types of place the vignettes cover. These include Bangladesh, Cameroon, Canada, Colombia, Democratic Republic of the Congo, Ghana, Indonesia, Mauritania, Mozambique, Myanmar/Burma, Nepal, Nigeria, Papua New Guinea, Sudan, and Thailand.

Finally, it is both a responsibility and a pleasure to acknowledge and thank our donors and some key individuals who have helped in special ways. To ensure that the lessons learned are publicly accessible, we have sought public funding in addition to the financial contributions of companies. We thank the World Bank and the governments of Canada, the Netherlands, the United Kingdom, Switzerland, and Germany for their financial and collegial support at various phases of the project.

In each of the site visits, we worked with various international and local experts who provided depth to the project's learning and placed our observations into their context. David Reyes led visits to Mozambique, Bangladesh, and Thailand and accompanied the team to Cameroon, Mauritania, and Colombia. Gary MacDonald led the CEP visit to the Democratic Republic of the Congo. Doug Fraser accompanied us to Papua New Guinea, Myanmar, and Canada, and Ana Paula do Nascimento joined visits to Myanmar and Thailand. The following people provided invaluable insights as team members during other visits: Sajeda Begum, Shawna Christianson, Simon Devung, Ibiba Don Pedro, Brian Ganson, Frederic Kama-Kama Tutu, Emma Nikki Owiredu, Akachukwu Nwankpo, Saubhagya Shah, Sonny Sukada, and Yezid Campos Zornosa.

Four colleagues with corporate experience read the manuscript and commented even as we sent it to the publisher for review. They deserve our special thanks for the time commitment they made and the perceptiveness and acuity of their specific suggestions and comments. These are Chris Anderson of Newmont Mining Corporation, James Austin of Harvard Business School, Ian Bannon of the World Bank, and Jean-Pierre Cordier of Total Professeurs Associés (retired from Total).

All of our CDA colleagues have provided immense support and discerning criticism through the months of our writing and all deserve our thanks for this. Particularly helpful throughout the months of evidence gathering, writing, editing, and the development of tools and graphics were Nicole Goddard and Andrew Yang. Much of the clarity of layout reflects their clever skills with ideas and technologies. Finally, Deborah Zawalich who, as Chief Finance Officer of CDA, really has no obligation to read manuscripts-in-progress, yet nonetheless spent precious hours reading, suggesting clarifications, and catching innumerable typographical errors, all of which have made the final manuscript both more readable and more accessible.

It would be a pleasure to blame any or all of these colleagues for mistakes that still appear in these pages but, alas, if such be there, they are our fault as their creators.

Luc Zandvliet, Director, Corporate Engagement Project
Mary B. Anderson, Executive Director, CDA Collaborative Learning Projects

Introduction

> " I am an engineer, not a sociologist. But sometimes I spend as much as 80% of my time dealing with crisis management and community problems. If you can help me reduce the time I spend on social issues, be my guest! "
>
> *(Company site manager)*

> " My company spends US$7 million per year on community programs. We still face work interruptions from the communities we help. Obviously the money does not buy us the goodwill we need, but I have no idea where we are missing the point."
>
> *(Managing director of an oil company)*

A not-uncommon short story

A company begins exploration of future operations in a remote and rural area of a poor but resource-rich country.

The communities in this area welcome the company's interest, seeing the prospects for improved social and economic conditions. They look forward to the creation of jobs and other income opportunities, and they look forward to being connected to the outside world through the company.

The company, for its part, wants to *get it right* with local communities. In order to understand the context in which they plan to operate as well as to demonstrate their respect for local mores, managers hire an anthropologist or a non-governmental organization (NGO) to do community surveys. They see these as the first steps for establishing good relations between the company and local communities.

Five years later, a visitor to the area sees schools and clinics that the company has built and staffed for the community. He sees upgraded roads and electricity that had not existed before. He sees increased activity in the region, more people, and more vehicles, as people have migrated to the area for work. But he hears the company manager complain that he spends far too much time dealing with the community's "never-ending demands" and with "local trouble-makers," and he hears community members complain that "the company has done nothing for us."

This book is for corporate managers who are responsible for company operations in societies that are poor and politically unstable. Many such managers — like those referred to above — are frustrated with the situations they face. They try their best to run effective, profitable, and beneficial operations that take account of the needs of all their stakeholders, including local surrounding communities. But, even with their best efforts, they encounter community dissatisfaction, unrest, opposition, delays, and, worse yet, threats and violence. This book is for managers who face such circumstances.

In many ways, this book is also written *by* such managers because the information and learning it includes come directly from their day-to-day, grounded field experience. For seven years, through the Corporate Engagement Project, we have spent days and weeks around the sites of over 60 companies that operate in a variety of locations around the world, talking with both company staff and local people. We have gathered the evidence of how the daily, ongoing operations of companies interact with, affect, and are affected by the societies where they work. We have heard lots of complaints — on both sides. We have seen policies and programs, intended to establish positive relations, backfire and, instead, bring angry demonstrations at the company gate and seemingly endless negotiations and demands. We have also seen operations that are appreciated and supported by local people because of the positive impacts they have had.

The short story above is one that, with small variations, CEP heard repeated again and again in different countries. Both corporations and communities begin their interactions with positive attitudes and expectations, but in a short time tensions between the two rise and negative attitudes surpass positive ones. In each location where CEP has seen this story play out there are, of course, variations and details that reflect the specific context and local history. But the regularity and similarity of complaints across so many contexts also show that there are clear, and predictable, patterns in the processes by which company–community relations turn sour.

The repetition could be discouraging, but it may also foretell possibilities. **When a process can be predicted, and its sources and mechanisms understood, it is likely that it can also be prevented.**

In this book, we report, analyze, and sort the broad and varied experience of many corporations, bringing forward the lessons that can be usefully applied in other settings. The purpose of this book is to help corporate managers **get it right** with respect to interactions with local communities, so that they can more efficiently and effectively accomplish their production goals and, at the same time, ensure that local communities are better (rather than worse) off as a result of their presence. The book also addresses what has been learned about how companies can interact, appropriately and positively, with national governments and advocacy NGOs in ways that promote, rather than undermine, the welfare of the citizens of the countries where they operate.

The evidence behind this book

The Corporate Engagement Project (CEP) was begun in 2000 by CDA Collaborative Learning Projects, Inc., a small non-profit agency based in Cambridge, Massachusetts, USA, that works with many international agencies involved in humanitarian, development, conflict-prevention, and peace-building activities. All of CDA's projects involve "collaborative learning" through which a broad range of international actors, together, gather their experiences and sort, analyze, and systematize what can be learned from this experience to improve future effectiveness.

Over the past seven years, the CEP has invited a broad range of international companies — especially those working in difficult circumstances where they often encounter problems with local communities, advocacy groups, and local governments — to become involved in the learning process. The purpose of this effort has been to gather the evidence of how companies and communities (and governments) interact and, by comparing this experience across many contexts and types of enterprise, to look for common patterns and generalizable trends. As the gathering of experience turns up patterns that are repeated in quite divergent circumstances, these provide insights and clues about how things too often go wrong in company–community relations and, also, about ways of improving future company–community interactions.

The evidence that this book reports is based on the experience of over 60 international companies operating in Africa, Asia, Latin America, Australia, and North America under difficult circumstances. It is evidence that is real and grounded. As CEP spent time in multiple countries in and around multiple corporate sites, we listened and watched and absorbed what was there to be gathered. As we began to see patterns and trends, we continually re-checked these with managers and local people in other locations to ask whether, and if so how, these patterns were familiar to them. As will become clear below, the evidence is primarily based on the experiences of extractive companies. Readers will judge for themselves how applicable these lessons are to other types of companies. Some of the examples may have relevance only to mining and energy companies, but most will, we believe, resonate with managers of many companies that work across borders.[1]

The specifics that we found were quite remarkable. Many companies and many communities have common experiences and shared frustrations. How these occur is not mysterious at all.

This book reports on this evidence and, by doing so, intends to help corporate managers see their own circumstances more clearly. The evidence in this book provides a backdrop of practical experience against which other corporate managers can analyze their own situations and, using what has been learned by smart colleagues before them, arrive at sound, practical approaches to their daily challenges.

No single problem – no single solution

When companies come into new areas to begin operations, both companies and communities want to **get it right**. Both start with high and positive expectations that they can work together harmoniously and gain from the relationship. Nonetheless, the relationship goes awry. Why does it happen and why does it keep happening?

Seldom is there one identifiable moment when someone does something so bad that this alone accounts for damage to otherwise healthy company–community relations. Seldom is it one thing that sours good relationships.

Most often, with good intentions and a focus on an immediate issue, individuals in companies and in communities take actions or make decisions (or fail to take actions or make decisions) that, over time, cumulatively and progressively add up to major problems. For this reason – alas – there is no single solution to the **getting it right** challenge. Rather, building strong cordial relations, or reversing a downward relational spiral, is a day-by-day, multi-step process. However, experience also shows that it is not mysterious or unfathomable. **Getting it right** is grounded in logical, sensible, and doable processes.

---

1 For more information about CDA, our approach to collaborative learning, the Corporate Engagement Project, and the companies involved, visit www.cdainc.com.

Why should a manager care?

Because neutrality is not an option

A mining manager states, "All we do is simply dig a hole in the ground," and by saying this, he signals his intention to stay out of politics and social issues. He defines his job as managing the engineering and business aspects of an operation; he sees social and political factors as outside his responsibility and as areas where he has no right to interfere.

Many managers intend to organize their operations so that they are technically efficient but have no effect on social, political, or conflict dynamics within the country. This is especially the case when a country has a long history of conflict. Corporate managers in such settings often feel overwhelmed by the complexity of the context, and they do not recognize the connections that are inevitable between the corporate presence and the local dynamics. They aspire to be neutral and to have no effect on what they see as basically external to their operations.

To get it right, managers must recognize that their policies and practices inevitably have impacts on social and political structures and relationships. Evidence shows that it is inevitable that some people gain from the corporate presence and some do not. It is inevitable that economic processes interact with power dynamics and decision-making processes. When societies are unstable or in conflict, external actors who enter these societies become a part of the society and, as such, their activities feed into, exacerbate, and prolong instability and conflict, or feed into, reinforce, and support systems that promote peace and stability. Even where corporate operations are separated from conflict by fences and guards, and even where operations are isolated, offshore, or located in remote areas, they have impacts on people's lives.

Corporate impacts can be either positive or negative, but, in any context of social or political tension, they are *never neutral*.

Company staff need to take this reality seriously as an intrinsic aspect of their jobs. Not to do so can reinforce destabilization of societies. Not to do so can increase resentments and even violence against a company, costing time and money in shutdowns, negotiations, and compensation.

Because the context of international corporate operations is changing

Beyond the immediate effects of corporate–community interactions, corporate managers also face growing scrutiny from the broader world. The scope, and the limits, of corporate accountability are in a period of rapid change, mostly in the direction of expansion. In the past decade, the world has been placing increasing demands on corporations for good citizenship and social responsibility. Pressures for companies to get it right in terms of community relations come from many levels.

The importance of ensuring local acceptance in order to exist is often discussed as gaining a social license to operate and is acknowledged by many managers. As one mining executive said, "If we cannot get it right above the ground, we cannot get to the stuff underground." Other companies acknowledge the importance of being "the company of choice" in new countries. Especially in the extractive industries, where mineral deposits in relatively stable contexts are being depleted, companies realize that, in a competitive market, a reputation for sound community engagement can be an important factor in an effort to obtain government approval for new projects.

Additional pressure on corporations comes from international advocacy groups, especially those concerned with human rights and economic inequality. With the availability of global technology, such groups can be aware of positive and negative social impacts of corporate activities anywhere in the world almost immediately.

Linkages can be established across groups operating at local and international levels via satellite and web connections. One manager, slightly nostalgic, observed "These days there are no far-away places anymore." As a result, advocacy groups have developed remarkable adeptness at naming and shaming corporate operations that they judge to be in violation of the values they advocate. When these international opinion-shaping organizations link up with disgruntled local communities in the areas of corporate projects, there can be global consequences for a company's reputation. Whereas historically companies only had to deal with local groups knocking on their gates, now they are confronted with global networks that mobilize media exposure and other forms of public scrutiny and criticism that can cost both time and money.

An emerging global expectation involves **user-chain responsibility**. The notion of supply-chain responsibility has been established for some years: for example, through initiatives that focus on labor practices in the garment industry. Increasingly companies are now expected also to take responsibility for how their products, assets, revenues, and legitimacy are used or abused. One oil company cancelled a contract with an air force after it became known that its product was used to fuel jets that allegedly bombed civilians. Other companies have suffered reputational damage when their airstrips or company vehicles were used by a local military for offensive purposes. Companies are regularly pressured to ensure that the revenues they help generate do not support oppressive governments. They are challenged when they are seen to provide legitimacy to governments that commit human rights violations.

With heightened awareness and increasing public scrutiny, international financial institutions such as the International Finance Corporation (IFC) and numerous private insurance and investment firms have also joined the overall trend to investigate and assess companies on their commitments to corporate social responsibility. Over 50 financial institutions have adopted the Equator Principles, which provide benchmarks for determining, assessing, and managing social and environmental risk in project financing. When advocacy groups push these financial institutions and sometimes join forces with them, companies can be sanctioned and find that sizable investment funds are withdrawn or withheld from their projects.

Finally, multinational bodies, such as the United Nations through its Global Compact, have also raised the bar for international corporations' sensitivity to local communities. Many professional associations, national bodies, and international groups have established codes of conduct, voluntary principles, and other forms of standards. Sometimes these protocols specify benchmarks that companies willingly accept as their own standard for assessment and accountability.

With attention and pressure from local communities to advocacy groups to multinational associations, corporate managers face a very different world and very different expectations from those they faced as recently as ten years ago. No longer is it possible for managers to claim that they *only* put a hole in the ground.

The world watches as companies operate and holds them to account for their broader impacts.

Many company managers (but unfortunately not all) agree with and welcome such accountability. Some resent the insinuation that they need to be prodded to care about their impacts on people's lives and that they are somehow less moral and less concerned for international standards than those who watchdog and pressure them.

Whatever the context, it is a fact of life that corporate operations are smoother and probably more profitable if and when the surrounding communities accept the companies' presence easily and without disruptions. With greater understanding of their interactions with local society, corporate managers can take decisions that make a difference to local communities and national governments. In the chapters that follow, we examine the evidence, and the options it opens, about how managers can navigate these decisions to ensure better outcomes. This book helps managers manage beyond the company gates. It also helps them manage their impacts on social and political realities.

How this book is organized

The following chapters are organized to help corporate managers see how the multi-layers of their operations interact to affect communities. In Section I, we start with an overview chapter that identifies three categories through which company policies and actions **get it right** or **get it wrong** in relation to communities. These categories provide the framework for analyzing, understanding, and ultimately predicting the impacts of all the aspects of a company's operations on local communities. Chapters 2, 3, and 4 then trace in more detail the three categories: benefits distribution, behavior, and side effects. Chapter 5 looks behind company actions to examine corporate assumptions that underlie these actions, and this is then followed by a special note on corporate operations in situations of conflict.

In Section II, seven chapters report on findings about how seven aspects of company operations affect community relations. These chapters cover: hiring, compensation, contracting, community consultation, community projects, working with advocacy NGOs, and working with governments. In these, we assemble many examples of field experiences that illustrate how company actions evoke varying responses from local people, advocacy groups, and host governments. The detail in these chapters is rich. Each context-specific example suggests ideas and options (some to be avoided, some to be pursued!) for other contexts. Looking at many examples from many locations will help company managers see their own circumstances more clearly, as these compare to and differ from those in the examples. In this section, following Chapter 9 on community consultation, we have included a special note on how to set up an effective grievance procedure, which, experience shows, is one critical aspect of establishing positive company–community relations.

In Section III, we then turn to a discussion of how the internal organization of a company interacts with, and too often reinforces, negative external relations. Again, examples are drawn from the broad experience gathered through CEP over the eight years of the project. And, again, these are illustrative – and suggestive – of possible pitfalls and opportunities available to corporate managers for organizing their management systems in support of, rather than undermining, positive external relations. These lessons are also of particular relevance for corporate headquarters where many of the internal operational systems are designed and perpetuated. Section III also includes a chapter on measuring effectiveness, which provides a summary overview of suggested indicators by which managers can assess the trends in company–community relations and, by being alert to small changes, prevent mistakes that lead to overall deterioration. Finally, we conclude in Chapter 15 with some reflections on how companies and individual managers can integrate the learning reported in the previous chapters into their immediate and daily work.

When a manager understands which elements of the company–community relationship are most important to communities and learns to recognize the indicators that these are (or are not) being effectively addressed, she or he will be able to develop approaches to operations that reinforce positive interactions and minimize negative impacts.

In closing

As we end this introduction we should reiterate. This book is for managers who are struggling to improve their company's relations with local communities in the areas where they operate. The experience and evidence assembled here will provide both a broad framework for understanding how things go wrong and how they go right and will illustrate these patterns with examples and details from many sites. The purpose is to enable managers to understand, predict, and track how company operations affect communities so they can ensure that both the company and communities benefit from their interactions.

As we trace the experience and outline what has been learned, we shall continue to push companies to accept accountability for the impacts of their policies and actions. This is not an ideological or academic exercise. Rather, all aspects of the findings in this book are based on evidence of how things work and why.

SECTION I

1

How to understand getting it wrong and getting it right
Toward a framework for analysis

Each location where CEP has worked with companies has characteristics shaped by its own particular geography, history, culture, environment, and economy. The importance of recognizing and appreciating the specifics of local contexts cannot be overemphasized. However, as the chapters in this section will show, we have seen amazingly clear commonalities surface again and again, across time and across locations. In fact, it is impossible *not* to see them!

That these commonalities — patterns — emerge from analyzing broad experience is heartening. It means that we can build on the past in ways that inform, and improve, future practice. We can take the learning from past experience and, by recognizing and applying these categories to future circumstances, go farther, faster in preventing and solving problems.

When CEP compared the experiences of companies across sectors and operating in different parts of the world, we found there are (only!) three areas that determine if companies **get it wrong** or if they **get it right** with respect to company–community relations. These areas are benefits distribution, behavior, and side effects.

In Figure 1.1 we introduce a framework for analysis of corporate–community relations to depict how these three areas can affect company–community relations either positively or negatively. The center column shows the three areas of interaction between companies and communities.

Figure 1.1 **Framework for analysis of corporate–community relations**

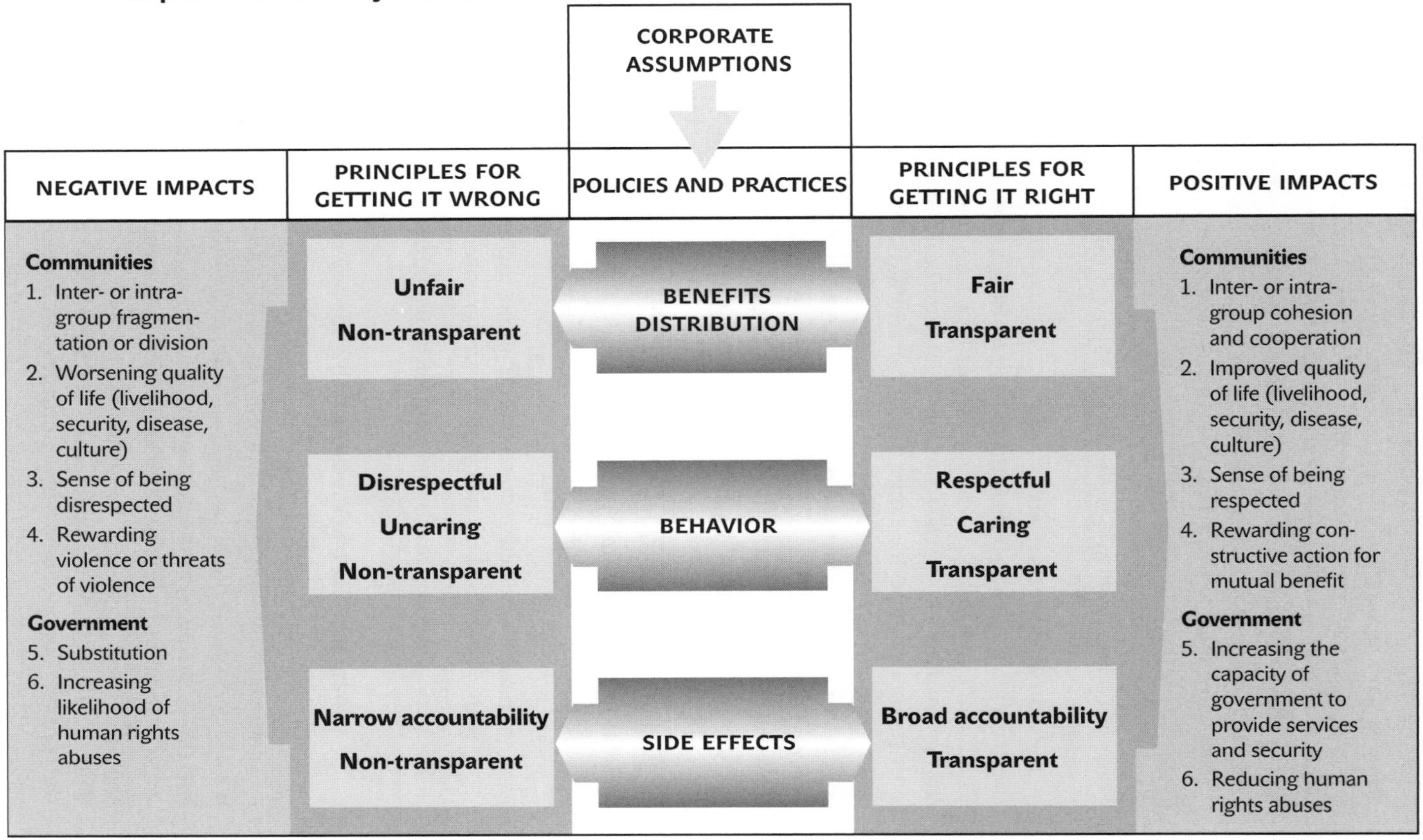

NEGATIVE IMPACTS	PRINCIPLES FOR GETTING IT WRONG	POLICIES AND PRACTICES	PRINCIPLES FOR GETTING IT RIGHT	POSITIVE IMPACTS
Communities 1. Inter- or intra-group fragmentation or division 2. Worsening quality of life (livelihood, security, disease, culture) 3. Sense of being disrespected 4. Rewarding violence or threats of violence **Government** 5. Substitution 6. Increasing likelihood of human rights abuses	**Unfair** **Non-transparent**	**BENEFITS DISTRIBUTION**	**Fair** **Transparent**	**Communities** 1. Inter- or intra-group cohesion and cooperation 2. Improved quality of life (livelihood, security, disease, culture) 3. Sense of being respected 4. Rewarding constructive action for mutual benefit **Government** 5. Increasing the capacity of government to provide services and security 6. Reducing human rights abuses
	Disrespectful **Uncaring** **Non-transparent**	**BEHAVIOR**	**Respectful** **Caring** **Transparent**	
	Narrow accountability **Non-transparent**	**SIDE EFFECTS**	**Broad accountability** **Transparent**	

CORPORATE ASSUMPTIONS

In the framework, **benefits distribution** refers to how tangible and intangible benefits such as wages, contracts, community projects, and legitimacy accrue to some people and not to others. How companies decide whom to employ (and whom not to employ), how to tender contracts, and how to interact with communities in other ways becomes a key challenge as it affects community dynamics and company–community relationships.

Behavior refers to the manner in which the company and company staff show respect, or lack of respect, for local people. It has to do with the signals that company policies and staff actions send to local people about trust, fear, and caring. Staff and company behaviors directly affect long-term company–community relationships.

The term **side effects** refers to the level of responsibility that a company takes for the broader and longer-term impacts that its presence has on local communities. This includes the influx of large groups of job seekers who descend on a host community, the effects on social cohesion of large amounts of money that flow into a host community, and the range of environmental problems that are introduced from corporate activities. Although in-migration and noise may seem to have little in common, we group them because companies are typically not legally required to address these side effects, but they do affect company–community relations.

Managers will recognize the importance of benefits distribution but may wonder why behavior and side effects are featured as equally important. The reason is that, when we systematically asked communities how they defined successful company–community relations, we heard remarkably consistent responses.

1. **Improved economic prospects and social services.** Included are: direct benefits from employment or contracts and indirect benefits from an improving quality of life (resulting from increased economic activity as well as better health, education, and infrastructure provided by the company or because a company brings greater government presence)

2. **A company approach that demonstrates fairness and respect**; a company that is a good neighbor

3. **A company that takes responsibility for any negative impacts** on people's lives that result from the corporate presence

Although many companies are acutely aware of the importance of the first category, they often overlook the last two categories, which are less tangible than the first. Local people are usually explicit about their hopes for jobs, contracts, and social services but begin to express their concerns about respect and caring and side effects only after they have negative experiences. However, for positive company–community relations, the latter categories are *no less important* than money and schools. This explains why companies can provide many economic benefits and social services and still find themselves in trouble with local communities!

How companies distribute benefits, behave, and handle side effects determines whether they get it right or get it wrong with communities, and whether they have positive impacts or negative impacts, also shown as columns in the framework. The ways in which benefits distribution, behavior, and side effects have right or wrong (positive or negative) impacts are noted in the columns. These are explained in full in the chapters that follow.

The framework also shows the essential principles of getting it right (and getting it wrong). For a company to get it right, benefits distribution needs to be fair, behavior needs to be respectful and caring, and the company must take broad responsibility for the side effects of its presence. In addition, a principle that crosses all categories as an essential factor in determining company–community relationships is **transparency**.

Transparency

Communities regularly say that they want more and better information from companies that operate in their regions. It is natural, and legitimate, for community members to want to know: Who are these people? What do they do? How do they live? How will they affect our lives?

Some company managers fear that transparency can put a company at a disadvantage. They worry that sharing too much information can strengthen opposition to company decisions or lead to more and increasingly unreasonable demands.

The evidence shows, however, that there are immediate benefits to be derived from policies and practices of transparency.

What does transparency do for a company? Why is it important?

Reinforces support from the community

Community representatives in a number of countries have said that they find they do not need to take strong and aggressive positions *vis-à-vis* company negotiations if their constituencies feel they know what can be expected from the company. Such knowledge comes from a sense that a company is open and honest — qualities that are demonstrated by transparent policies and practices. Transparency can also reinforce the legitimacy of community leaders who work with (rather than against) a company because they are seen to be well informed.

Lowers demands and supports better long-term planning

Some community members have told CEP that, because they had no idea of how a company's presence would affect their lives over time, they took a short-term, demanding approach to negotiations with the company. In retrospect they say that, had they had more information about company plans, they would have taken a more conciliatory approach and avoided some of the early community–company tensions.

Identifies issues early before they become problems

Established systems of regular and open communication that are part of a transparent approach can draw out concerns of communities before these grow into grievances. Regular and comfortable meetings provide one of the few non-hostile and non-violent settings in which companies can be alerted to potential problems in time to deal with them easily.

Counters rumors

Transparency can prevent and counter rumors about a company. When people feel as if they know enough, and are comfortably certain that the company will keep them informed on issues that matter, they are less prone to join campaigns against the company. When managers speak with community representatives in public and on the record, rather than behind closed doors, this quells speculation that some deals are being made and some people are receiving special favors.

Signals honesty, trust, and respect

Finally, openness — both the fact of openness and the signal from a company that it intends to be open and above board — reassures a community from the beginning that they will be aware of plans and problems that may affect them. In this way, transparency establishes a basis of relationship that is grounded in honesty and forthrightness. Alternatively, when companies are not transparent, communities fear that such secrecy covers insincerity, dishonesty, and trickiness.

Transparency about what?

To many people, a company's intent and practice of openness are more important than the content of the information shared. In general, communities do not want to know everything about a company. Instead, they want to see that the company is willing to share information when asked and that it makes efforts to keep communities informed.

People say they are not after sensitive, proprietary information. Rather, they want to understand the day-to-day operations of a company, including even such mundane things as the number of cars the company has, what the production process looks like, or what kind of food is served in the company canteen!

Other more important issues are also named. For example, almost everyone says that communities need and deserve to know exactly how jobs are allocated. They want transparency about the criteria that determine who gets employment or that determine which communities get community projects. Of particular importance to communities is information about potential negative impacts of a company's presence and the company's plans for addressing these. Clear, available publicity about these issues can save a company from multiple community challenges and support healthier community–company relations.

Communities also tell CEP that they want honesty about what is and is not feasible. If people do not know what managers can and cannot agree to, they will push for more. Most communities find this method of testing limits as frustrating as managers find it. They would prefer transparent and open conversations about roles and limits that are based in fact and are not defensive. One manager who discussed limits of what the company could do for the community said that the community told him, "We disagree with everything you say, but it is the first time that the company has been honest with us!"

Of course for real transparency, companies need to explain *and* to listen. Sometimes communities have imaginative ideas that managers simply have not considered, and these may offer solutions for what seemed to be intractable problems.

Getting all the parts right

We should note now, and will continue to do so below, that the three areas – benefits distribution, behavior, and side effects – need to be understood and addressed together. Experience shows that it is not good enough to get benefits distribution right and simultaneously fail to address issues included in the behavior or side effects columns. Even if a company develops a completely fair system of distributing benefits, if it operates in a non-transparent way getting benefits distribution right will not overcome getting behavior wrong. Similarly, a company can be completely open, honest, and transparent and bring immediate benefits to a location but, if it takes no responsibility for any of the negative side effects that occur when a company starts up activities in a poor region, communities will not be satisfied that the company is a good neighbor.

On the other hand, experience shows that, when a company distributes benefits in a transparent, fair, and inclusive manner, behaves respectfully, demonstrates a caring approach, and takes broad responsibility for the side effects of its presence, it has positive impacts on local communities. In the framework, positive and negative impacts are grouped into six categories (depicted in the two impacts columns in Fig. 1.1). Four of these are direct community impacts and two are related to the government's impacts on people's lives.

The next three chapters discuss benefits distribution, behavior, and side effects. In each of these chapters, we bring together the experience of companies that have gotten it wrong and of companies that have gotten it right using the four principles of transparency, fairness, respect, and broad responsibility for side effects. From these experiences, we are able to outline general guidelines that can be used by managers in similar situations around the world for better outcomes.

The final chapter in this section looks at what we have learned about how a company's assumptions shape (sometime mis-shape) policies and practice — also for better or for worse. Assumptions affect the principles by which a company chooses to distribute benefits, rewards certain kinds of behavior, and determines the level of responsibility for side effects.

2

Benefits distribution
Getting it wrong and getting it right

The benefits distribution issue

The first category for understanding and analyzing company–community relations is benefits distribution.

Both communities and companies expect that the tangible benefits – jobs, salaries, contracts, roads, and other infrastructure – that come from company operations will contribute to positive company–community relations.

Communities expect that a company's presence will benefit some people directly and all people in the communities indirectly. That is, they expect that individuals will get jobs or contracts or compensation payments that will be of direct benefit to them. They also expect that the people who do not get a job or a contract or do not sell their land to the company will also find their lives and their livelihood prospects indirectly improved as a result of the company's impact on the overall economy. Communities also recognize that there are intangible benefits from a company's arrival. They see that the way a company does its business can influence community–government relations as well as internal community power relationships by legitimizing activities and people through involving them in company operations. Many local communities also report that they benefit from a sense of connectedness to the outside world when an international company locates in their area. Communities value the intangible benefits from a company's presence as well as the tangible benefits.

For their part, companies normally calculate their transactions in material terms, citing costs and benefits, investments and returns. Company managers expect to

pay for land, workers, contractors, and other assets they need to support their operations, and they assume that there is a price (a *fair* price) at which they will be able
to acquire these things. They are also concerned with anticipating and minimizing
risks that can arise from opposition to their operations so they expect to provide
services and/or infrastructure to local communities that will ensure that they are
welcome. They make such investments assuming that these will pay off in terms of
goodwill among communities. In both direct payments and community investments, managers want to keep the costs of doing business reasonable. In deciding
how to allocate company benefits to individuals and communities, managers regularly monetize their choices, seeking to ensure both smooth operations and satisfactory profit margins.

However, how a company distributes benefits can work either positively or negatively in terms of company–community relations. Too often, through three very
predictable processes, benefits distribution becomes a negative factor, causing disruptions and anger among local communities. We now explain how this occurs
and then explore what a company needs to know and do to get benefits distribution
right.

Getting it wrong with benefits distribution

It may seem odd that something as positive as benefits can have a negative impact.
Are "benefits" not beneficial? The answer is, "Not always. Not necessarily. And not
for everyone."

Experience shows that the negative effects of benefits distribution follow three
prominent patterns: unfair exclusive criteria, dividers and connectors, and rewarding violence.

Unfair exclusive criteria

It is easy to understand that the distribution of company benefits (tangible and
intangible) to some people and not to others can feed into competition and jealousy
among individuals and communities and can heighten tensions between communities and companies. It is easy also to anticipate that the way that benefits are distributed – how priority groups are chosen, for example – can be complicated when
many people are poor and all are eager to gain from a company's presence.

Indeed, the single most troublesome issue that companies face in benefits distribution is the resentment that communities feel when they think that the *wrong* people gain a lot while other *deserving* people get nothing. This, communities say, is
unfair.

Of course, companies respond that they simply cannot (and should not) hire everyone or give contracts to all bidders; they should not pay compensation to people or provide community projects to those whose lives they do not negatively affect. People need to *qualify* for work, compensation payments, and contracts. And communities agree. They are aware of and comfortable with the fact that some people will gain more from a company's presence than others, and they recognize that not everyone can get a job or a contract. Straight equality is not, they say, their standard of fairness.

> Managers often define fairness according to market economics

Experience shows that companies repeatedly pursue approaches to benefits distribution that they believe to be fair but that are seen by communities to be intrinsically unfair. Sometimes a problem arises because company managers define fairness according to market economics, believing that anything of value can command a price that is fair and appropriate. This mind-set leads managers to approach benefits distribution as a transaction rather than an aspect of relationship building. Sometimes problems can occur because communities simply do not know why certain groups get more benefits than others; they do not know the criteria. When communities do not have clarity about the criteria companies use, they question the fairness of the process.

For example, companies often designate the communities they will deal with as those that are most affected by immediate operations. If a community is affected, managers will transact with it to provide benefits that offset negative effects. In addition, they focus their community relations and community service programs in this same area where they are providing the most direct compensation to families who give up land or who are otherwise directly inconvenienced by company operations. This is also the area that gains the most in infrastructure improvements of roads, water supplies, and power supplies, because the company needs these for its own use.

However, such designations are always arbitrary. They inevitably leave out other, often nearby, communities. A narrow designation of who falls within the cared-for zone, and who falls outside it, leads local communities to compare benefits and to compete for company attention, sometimes through negative interactions.

In one country, a company was so concerned about relating well to the people within its quite large operational zone that it even built a model village with a world-class hospital and school. Communities at some distance told the visiting CEP team that, as soon as the company left this region, there would be "payback" time. They said they would go into this area and take what they wanted because "those people got so much" over the years of the company's operations. Recent reports from the area indicate that these threats have turned into actions and are disrupting company operations that are still ongoing.

Similarly, managers believe it is fair to hire on merit. However, when local people consistently do not have the specified qualifications for jobs, so that outsiders get the jobs, the definition of merit is seen by communities as unfair.

Unfairness extends to still other characteristics. When an individual who has political connections or who is in some position of power that could disrupt company functions gets a better job, or is kept on even though he misses work and does not do the job well, communities see this as unfair. They become disgruntled when someone who does not deserve employment gets it and keeps it, when others who are more deserving but who do not have the same leverage with the company are left out.

When a community sees that a company distributes its benefits unfairly, this contributes to negative and deteriorating company–community relations. The other two predictable patterns of negative benefits distribution, discussed below, are directly related to and are sub-components of the unfairness factor.

Dividers and connectors: pre-existing relations among groups[2]

An area of unfairness that deserves special attention by managers has to do with pre-existing relations among identity groups who benefit from the company's presence and those who do not benefit from it.

All humans have a range of identities. Ethnicity, tribe, religion, political beliefs, sex, age, income level, neighborhood, village, clan, interests, history, and so on (and on) provide the bases for people's identities. People generally feel connected to others who share their identities, and when these identities are broadly shared across societies, people tend to live and work together cooperatively.

However, in many situations, identities have historically provided a basis for discrimination or preferential treatment. In such places, individuals often emphasize their sub-identities that set them apart from groups who have other characteristics. Where this occurs, intergroup tensions, rivalries, and conflict (sometimes with violence) are common. In societies where there is intergroup conflict, would-be leaders often gain popular support by appealing to and exacerbating divisions based on people's sub-identities. They convince people that their sub-group is under threat from other groups and that it is important to oppose those other groups. People contending for leadership thereby encourage the formation of sub-groups that emphasize the factors that divide, rather than connect, people.

---

2   Dividers and connectors analysis was developed by CDA's Do No Harm Project, and is covered in full in Mary B. Anderson, *Do No Harm: How Aid Can Support Peace – Or War* (Boulder, CO: Lynne Rienner Publishers, 1999). The CEP has found this analysis applies directly to corporate operations in areas where there are pre-existing intergroup tensions.

When a company enters an area, its actions affect sub-groups differently. When a company acts in ways that highlight and reward differences among groups, dividers can be worsened. When a company acts in ways that reinforce and reward common interests across groups, connectors are strengthened.

What kinds of thing might company managers look for to understand dividers and connectors in the communities that surround their operations?

There is no universal set of factors that divide people or connect them. In every society, there are always both connectors and dividers. People may be divided by wealth levels but connected by religion or history or beliefs. They may be divided by religion but connected by shared trade and markets. They may be divided by geography but connected by ethnicity. There are many variations in both dividers and connectors.

However, managers should always be aware that both dividers and connectors do exist, and they should always find out what these are in order to predict the impacts of company operations on them.

When a company acts in ways that inadvertently benefit people who are from one sub-group and create disadvantages for people from another sub-group, especially if there have been tensions between these two groups prior to the company's intervention, the impacts of company decisions very likely will — without any intention to do so — exacerbate the hostility between these groups. CEP experience shows that companies affect dividers and connectors through compensation, hiring, stakeholder consultation, contracting, and social investment policies.

We should note that community relations programs, intended to support positive company–community relations also can be divisive. They often inadvertently feed into and worsen intergroup conflict rather than recognizing, building on, and reinforcing intergroup connectors. Building a school in one area for one group, especially if this group has previously been in conflict with other surrounding groups, can heighten tensions. Where one locates community projects, whom one hires to build or staff them, whom they are intended to serve, who decides where these are built, by whom and for whom — all of these aspects of community relations programs also interact with existing dividers and connectors and, as such, can have negative (or positive) impacts on intergroup relations within recipient societies.

Focus on commonalities, not differences

A careful manager was eager to establish positive relations with local communities so he hired an anthropologist to do an extensive survey of the community prior to the project's start-up. The anthropologist reported that there were seven major tribes in the area and 23 sub-tribes. She also outlined the importance of tribal identities as they influenced social and political relations. Intending to signal his desire to establish respectful relations with local people, the manager decided to negotiate all pertinent issues, such as land usage and compensation policies, with each of the 23 sub-tribes rather than with the seven major tribes, or even all tribal leaders as a single group.

Over time it became clear that the well-intentioned decision to honor each sub-tribe through separate negotiations led local people to emphasize their differences rather than their common interests. This approach also tied the company's management up in endless negotiations as each group vied to get more compensation than all the others. Things got worse over time because local people, realizing benefits might be gained through division, split the 23 sub-tribes into smaller groups who claimed to have special differences and needs. In a few cases, the emphasis on differences rather than on connections was a contributing factor to intergroup violence.

Some years later in a return visit to the area, the manager asked a group of men who had become quite wealthy through the individualized compensation approach what they, in hindsight, would suggest he should have done differently. As a group and without hesitation, they answered that rather than negotiating separately with multiple groups, the company should have established a community-wide trust fund. Although individual homeowners would have needed to be compensated for the loss of their homes and land, the major company payments (these men said) should have gone into such a trust to support community-wide activities that benefited all groups together.

Rewarding violence

Related to unfairness, but with additional dimensions, are company actions that inadvertently reward violence.

Inevitably, when a company begins operations, local people want to be in touch with the manager about issues and problems that arise. They want someone in the company who can hear what they have to say and deal with them, someone who can make decisions. They write letters or try to visit. However, too often, they cannot get an appointment, and they get no response to their letters. They begin to get frustrated and, after some time, frustration turns into grievance. Then, to get the company's attention, people threaten to, or actually do, block the road, demonstrate at the plant gate, close down the pumping station, or cut the pipeline. What they want is to talk about what concerns them and to find a joint company–community solution.

However, when a company is threatened, a typical response is either to call in the army or police to control the people or to enter negotiations with the community.

The first option always leads to increased community resentment and anger. Communities that have been attacked by a company's security guards (or by the army on behalf of a company) are ripe for organizing into groups hostile to the company. They are ready to participate in direct action or violence.

The second option involves the distribution of benefits with a negative impact. When a company offers payments or community projects in response to threats, communities see this as a direct reward for aggression. When people who are violent receive undue attention and benefits, there is a general sense that the company is treating most people — that is, those who are not violent — unfairly and distorting systems by which rewards have traditionally be decided.

When people see communities that are violent toward a company receiving direct cash payments or community projects, this motivates them to threaten the company. Their frustration at not being able to have a reasonable conversation with a company manager, coupled with their observation that others receive benefits through violence, moves them also to violence. When direct confrontations result in higher and higher "buyoffs" through contract awards or in projects such as schools, clinics, credit schemes, and the like, communities will, with some rationale, resort to violence.

What begins as an attempt to calm a specific crisis can easily become an ensconced way of doing business. In one volatile area visited by CEP, anyone who could mobilize a group of 15 young people could claim to be a youth leader and demand "contracts" from companies. In this region, elders reported that new youth groups formed every few months. The youth leaders reported that they saw their village elders getting payoffs from a company to control the people so they, therefore, took up violence against corporations in order to get in on such cash payments. Companies responded with a policy of appeasement, hiring these groups to protect company assets from attacks by other youth groups. In essence, a system that was developed as a method of payoffs in response to threats and vandalism became accepted by everyone as a legitimized contract system.

The community initially saw this system as unfair — that is, rewarding people who did not deserve to be rewarded. Once it became ensconced as a way of doing business, even those who gained by threatening the company, although they had not wanted to do so in the first place, began to feel that it was only fair, because the company would not deal with them in any other way.

> ❝ When we saw that the youth of that neighboring village who blocked the road were then hired by the company to protect it from their own threats, so they got both jobs and income, this looked good. We would be fools just to sit here and wait. For what? ❞
>
> *Woman from a rural village*

Company policies and practices that risk rewarding violence or obstructive behavior

- More community projects to the more difficult communities
- No systematic response to letters with complaints or non-violent expressions, but immediate response to threats and closedowns
- Non-inclusive distribution of benefits (e.g., only to the nearest communities)
- Compensation approaches that upset traditional systems
- Contracts to local groups to "protect" assets

Most companies define security in terms of their own staff and assets and do not consider how their actions – specifically decisions about how to distribute benefits – affect relations among local people and their security or insecurity. As the discussions on dividers and connectors and on rewarding violence show, the way a company acts in its day-to-day operations has direct effects on the likelihood of violence among groups as well as against the company. Company programs, including the community relations programs intended to gain favor with local communities, directly affect the probability that groups will either fight with each other or solve differences without violence and that they will either threaten the company or work with it peacefully. These benefits distribution issues constitute the first category through which company operations can have a negative impact.

Getting it right with benefits distribution

So what does a manager do to get the benefits distribution part of company operations right? In the discussion of getting it wrong, the right approaches are implied.

The principle of fairness in benefits distribution

A right approach to benefits distribution is based on the principle of **fairness**. Fairness refers to how people in communities perceive the distribution of benefits and their share of these.

As noted, communities expect two levels of benefit from a company's presence: individual direct payments and collective indirect advantages. Both of these should be seen to be fair. Every society has its own understanding of what is, and is not, acceptable in terms of resource differences. All societies tolerate some degree of inequality among individuals and groups (and most have systems for taking care of people who do not have enough to survive).

Equitable distribution – not equal distribution – is the standard of fairness.

Communities appreciate a company that acknowledges their existing value systems and the processes they have for ensuring that people are not too rich or too poor. Further, they welcome systems that ensure that nobody gains more than his or her share from the company's presence. Essentially what matters, people say, is that deserving people get what they deserve and those who do not deserve rewards do not get them.

> Communities expect two levels of benefits from a company: individual and collective. Both need to be fair and need to be seen to be fair

Further, many communities assign value to immaterial and intangible things such as historical and traditional hierarchies, social relations, and spiritual qualities. These, they say, cannot be compensated for with money. Because they do not put a price on all aspects of their lives, the benefits they expect and value are multi-layered. Managers need to ensure that people feel they receive non-monetary benefits, as well as payments, as a result of a company's presence.

Figuring out how to work within the valuation system and the understanding of fairness of the local community is one of the real challenges that company managers face as they work to get it right in their relationships with communities.

What does fairness do for a company? Why is it important?

Reassures about disruption

When a company signals that it wants to be fair and that it intends to work within the systems that define fairness in the local setting, it reassures community members that it respects their ways of doing things and that it will not disrupt pre-existing relationships.

Reduces needless competition and fear

If, from their very first interactions, a company convinces local communities that it intends to work within the system that these communities understand as fair, individuals, families, and clans can enter into negotiations on compensation or apply for jobs and contracts without having to pit their success against the failure of others.

Reinforces the long-term view over short-term gains

A company's commitment to fairness signals that, if later negative impacts emerge from the company's actions, people will be listened to and responded to. They will not be allowed to become long-term losers.

Fairness about what?

As noted, communities care both about how benefits are distributed among individuals and groups for equitable (but not strictly equal) results, and about how, as communities, they feel fairly rewarded for having let the company come into their area. These two dimensions, fairness in relative benefits and fairness in collective benefits, are intertwined, and attention to both will prevent community disgruntlement and destructive competitiveness.

In an African oil region, communities living in poverty feel entitled to a fair share of the benefits that "their" oil generates. This entitlement is a collective one, superseding the multiple individual and sub-group claims that get so much media attention. Communities in this area are dismayed that they see a disproportionate amount of the wealth leaving the oil-producing area where they continue to struggle for survival.

> ❝ Look at Saudi Arabia. They have sand and oil and still can make ice rinks in the desert. Look at us. We have fertile soil and oil. Still, we drink water out of polluted streams. All our oil gets stolen by big companies and corrupt politicians in the capital. ❞

> *(Receptionist of an oil company in Africa)*

A second aspect of fairness that regularly arises has to do with how companies and communities define what it means to be local. Companies commit themselves to giving preference to local people in hiring and contracting. Communities agree that this is important for fairness but are also clear that they do not expect or want only locals to benefit from a company's operations. Getting inside the definitions of local in any community is an additional important challenge for company managers who strive to be fair.

How can a manager get fairness right?

1. Ask communities how they understand or define fairness

The most important step in getting it right is to ask communities what they see as fair. Who do they consider local and why? What do they see as determining that a person deserves compensation, or not? Why? Asking these straightforward questions can yield essential ideas, as well as goodwill.

Sometimes what is fair as it relates to company benefits is not culturally fixed but will need to be talked through and agreed to by communities. Getting communities to define what they will accept as fair in relation to a company's operations is a rule for ensuring that the company's approaches match the fairness definitions of communities.

Fairness in the long term

A mining company agreed with communities in the direct vicinity of its plant to make all communities from the larger mine concession area, rather than a smaller mine-take area, eligible for local jobs. The communities who were located closest to the company acknowledged that, if they allowed outside people to qualify for local jobs, they — the local people — would also qualify for other jobs in the future if the company opened other mines in the larger area. This was perceived to be a fair arrangement by all these communities.

2. Be transparent about why certain groups receive more benefits than others and what criteria are applied

People need to understand a company's procedure for allocating benefits. They need to know how they can gain access to these benefits or why they are not eligible. Companies therefore need both to announce all benefits to be distributed (such as jobs or contracting opportunities) clearly and widely, and to publicly announce who has received company benefits and why those people qualified while others did not.

Transparency can lead to self-monitoring

One company used public bulletin boards in communities to name the farmers eligible to collect crop compensation money. Local residents noticed names of people who did not farm at all. They informed the company of the illegitimate claims and the compensation policy was reviewed. This transparent approach reduced the number of illegal claims and the cost to the company.

3. Understand that fairness relates to non-material as well as material benefits

Communities, assessing whether the presence of a company makes their community better off or worse off, very often calculate the benefits to the community — the collective benefits — in non-material ways. When companies work with communities to advocate for government interventions that communities have not been able to secure without company support, people see this as a definite — and collective —

non-material benefit. The overall calculation of benefits and their fairness has multiple layers. Successful managers acknowledge those benefits that lie beyond monetized or material things.

In an area where people did not trust their national government, one individual said,

> " We are able to sleep at night because the company provides a brake on government violence. The company management has access to the big ears in the capital city and, when things go wrong, they can make a telephone call to correct them. "

4. Engage with many people

When companies consult with a broad range of people, they are perceived to be interested in and open to the full range of opinions, and they can get a good overview of the range of interests and positions that exist in a community. Even when choices must be made between differing opinions, people feel they have had a fair hearing in the decision-making process.

5. Support connectors, minimize dividers

A dividers and connectors analysis of the local situation can guide a manager to emphasize and reinforce common and collective interests. A first step is to ask people to describe the things that link them to others. CEP has seen that this can reveal fascinating connectors that were not obvious even to local people until they were asked about them. Managers should ensure that no policy, decision, or action — especially with regard to jobs, contracts, community projects, and other means that confer material benefits or legitimacy — delivers all benefits to one identity group where there are existing intergroup tensions.

6. Generate widely shared and widely enjoyed benefits

A company's resource allocations can serve as a means of bringing groups together and generating widely enjoyed benefits. One way to make this happen is to engage with representatives of larger, rather than smaller, identities and to focus on issues and interests that people have in common. If a company helps local people start income-generating activities in the area of its operations, it can also help them link these activities to distribution systems, processing systems, export systems, etc., that create a network of interconnected economic enterprises across a larger geographic area. In this way, the localized company-sponsored benefits spread and link to other regions and an inclusive set of communities.

Maintaining peace can be a powerful connector

An oil company feared violence between communities (and, therefore, company–community conflict) over employment, contracts, and community projects as it began to implement a new major project. Correspondingly, all communities in the area realized that, if the company focused exclusively on the community nearest to its operations, this focus would prompt violence from those who were excluded from company benefits.

Anticipating problems that would arise from exclusivity, the company and the communities agreed to engage an independent mediator to negotiate a benefits-distribution agreement among all the communities based on population size, ancestral ownership, and the degree of disruption they would experience during construction.

Negotiations took place in three stages: first, consultation with traditional rulers; second, establishment of the principles that would guide final negotiations with the three dominant communities; and, third, a final set of negotiations with all stakeholders including all communities, the company, government representatives, and contractors.

The project was implemented without any conflict among communities or between communities and the company, and it was completed with zero down days from community unrest.

7. Reward reasonable and thoughtful interaction, not violence

The discussion above about how companies inadvertently reward violence suggests another getting-it-right approach — namely, that managers should interact early and consistently with non-violent and reasonable communities, and non-violent and reasonable people within communities. Company managers who signal their readiness to engage in a thoughtful process to correct problems as soon as issues arise reassure communities that reasonable interactions will be rewarded more than threats and violence.

Companies that develop systems to respond immediately and openly to non-violent inquiries and complaints are recognized as treating communities fairly. A simple way for managers to convey their concern with fairness is to intentionally call on and respond to the quiet people in community meetings as much as to those whose voices are the loudest and most demanding. This approach will legitimize thoughtful community engagement and show it to be effective, and it will delegitimize threats and violence as techniques for getting the company's attention. In total, such actions will enable a manager not to be sucked into a spiral of rewarding benefits to troublesome groups.

Conclusion

Getting it wrong and getting it right in benefits distribution is not mysterious. However, it does require that managers see their decisions in a new light — seeking to be fair in the terms that local people define. Additionally, it requires that managers engage consistently with the non-threatening and reasonable people in local communities rather than with trouble-makers and that they allocate benefits (material and non-material) in ways that build on and reinforce shared interests and benefits rather than in ways that divide people. These principles make sense. They have been seen to affect company–community relations directly and profoundly. Handling the management of benefits distribution is the first category by which a company establishes the positive — or negative — tone of its company–community relations.

3

Corporate behavior
Getting it wrong and getting it right

The behavior issue

The second category for understanding and analyzing company–community relations is behavior.

If a company provides jobs, builds roads, and supports communities, why do behaviors matter? Whose behaviors? Which behaviors? Where? When? The answers to these questions are more encompassing than most managers recognize. Communities tell us that the way a company acts, through the daily actions of its staff and its institutional stance, communicates how much the company cares, or does not care, about the community. They say that behaviors send implicit messages about respect and disrespect, about trust and mistrust, and about caring or non-caring.

These implicit messages are conveyed through the ways that company personnel *act* – in their public and private time, on the job and off, in villages, public meetings, cafes, shops, and golf courses. It may seem unreasonable to expect company staff to be on display and on duty at all times, but, more often than we can report, CEP has heard local communities speak about the behavior of company staff as a central factor that affects their attitudes toward a company. They describe how such actions can make them angry, or willing to cooperate, with a company.

Further, people say that a company's institutional behaviors also communicate whether or not it cares about the community. Some company actions – and modes of interacting – are insulting; others show respect. Some show suspicion; others convey trust. Some show indifference; others communicate caring.

Company managers, on their side, entrust their external affairs and public relations departments with the job of managing their messages. They rely on carefully worded communiqués to inform their stakeholders about who they are and how they work. They publish brochures and reports and codes of conduct and statements of principle to communicate how they feel about and intend to interact with communities. However, experience shows that more messages are communicated to local communities by company behaviors than by words or publications. Managers often overlook or ignore these more nebulous, but critically important, factors that shape community perceptions and attitudes when their company locates in others' societies and cultures.

When communities claim that companies do not respect them or care about them, or that they cannot trust the company, managers find this unsettling. They cannot measure — or even assess — trust, caring, or respect. They have no systems for programming around these intangibles. What can a manager do with this? Some of the answers to this problem will be addressed in subsequent chapters where we discuss community consultation. But one very direct and immediate way to understand community resentments over intangible feelings is to think about which messages are sent by official, and unofficial, staff actions. Underlying this understanding·is recognition that behaviors evoke mirroring, or corresponding, behaviors.

Getting it wrong with behavior

Maintaining distance, emphasizing security

When the face of a company is represented by armed guards at the gate and barbed wire around the compound, and entry by local people is forbidden, the message to local communities is a hostile, and separating, one. When senior company managers never show their faces in the community but expect community representatives to come to them, they send a message of aloofness and superiority. When company staff drive in large, fast-moving, and defensively outfitted vehicles, with radio antennae sprouting from their hoods and mesh protecting their windshields, communities get the message that company people do not trust them and that they are afraid of them. When people feel mistrusted and feared, they wonder what the company needs to hide. Fear begets fear; mistrust begets mistrust. And, clearly, fear and mistrust do not provide a basis for healthy interactions.

Company policies and practices that assume people will try to con the company and milk it for all it is worth will evoke trickery and greed. When a company begins negotiations with a community citing legal regulations and precedents (even though these may in fact be relevant and useful at some point in the conversation), or when staff seem to be suggesting technical solutions to community concerns, people perceive this as disrespect for existing cultural values and systems.

A company that keeps its distance has no human face to which community people can relate. The entity is seen as large, rich, and disembodied. Without a personal relationship, communities find it easy to imagine the worst, and they feel few constraints on their own behaviors against such a force. The language of community–company interactions becomes one of intimidation, threat, and possibly violence.

Rushing, deciding for, delivering to

Many communities that surround company operations complain that they do not feel respected. They specifically name the behaviors of companies and company staff that convey this lack of respect.

'My time is more valuable than yours . . .'

The company's community relations officer sped through the several villages he was to visit that day. He laughed as he described how he always wanted to be a race car driver. "People in the villages know they had better scatter when I come through because of how I drive." In one village, an elderly man flagged him down. He stopped, motor running, in the middle of the road and rolled down his window. The man approached, bowing slightly, and asked a question about the promised new roofing for the school. The community relations officer answered directly and quickly, reassuring the man that the plans were in place for this delivery. He then sped on.

The community relations officer had done his job. He had arranged for and followed through on the community school project that had been negotiated with the company. However, his style — the fact that he expected the community to scatter for him as he indulged his driving fantasy — expressed disrespect. He did not arrange a community meeting to report back on the roofing plans. He expected a community member to wait by the side of the road until he came by and to flag him down so that, without getting out of the car, he could talk briefly. The message was that his time was more valuable than the time of the villagers. His actions said that he was in a rush and they could have only a small moment of his important day. He wondered why the demands for more and more things kept coming, and his boss wondered why they continued to get negative feedback from surrounding communities even when the company did so much for them.

This category of unintended negative messages is broad. Company staff can schedule a meeting with a community and, by this, intend to send the explicit message that the community is important to the company. However, if they fidget and look uncomfortable, if they explain things in a condescending way, if they respond only to men (or to women, or to trouble-makers) and not to everyone, their actions send implicit messages of superiority, impatience, unease, and disrespect. In one area, a man told CEP that the value of a community–company meeting that was going very well was completely undermined when the company representative kept looking at his watch. The community found this insulting and disrespectful.

Communities have often told us of the disrespect they feel when a company decides what they need and then provides it. "Of course we wanted this bridge," said one community, "But we did not want the company to decide it for us. We don't use it because it is not our bridge; it is the company's." Managers describe the empty schools, the unused clinics, and the unmaintained wells that they have provided to communities, sometimes with wonderment. Communities report that the delivery of these things has been done with complete disregard for the process. They see that the company delivers things because they want to buy peace, or because they want to take a photograph of what they have given. They conclude, "The company does not care about us."

Managing information, communicating to (not with)

When a company does not engage with local people as partners in decision making and therefore limits the information it is willing to share to what it considers safe for people to know, communities recognize this as information management and resent the mistrust and disrespect its implies. When companies are more concerned with the messages they want to deliver to communities than with the messages that communities want to deliver to them, they are seen to be arrogant and uncaring. When companies keep information to themselves and are not transparent, communities fear that this secrecy represents insincerity, dishonesty, and trickiness.

Managers who explain company processes in technical terms that local people do not understand do not convince local people of their sincerity and concern for their well-being. Managers who bring a legal advisor to the meeting where they propose to decide on company–community commitments is seen to be self-protective rather than interested in mutually beneficial processes and outcomes.

> ᵉᵉ This company kept telling us that the content of the sludge they pumped into the sea was not harmful. They kept using these ppm figures, which I don't understand. No matter how much scientific terminology they use, I don't believe them. The water smells different from before and there are not as many shrimps as there used to be. To me, a

good indicator of improvement is to have green growing in the beach area where grass used to grow but then died because of that sludge. "

(Village woman)

A manager who does not engage in genuine discussion (and may appear to always agree, without sincerity, to things that local people say) is seen, local people tell us, as paternalistic and condescending, conveying the message, "These people are too limited to understand my sophisticated thinking so I will not try to explain it." The failure by individual company staff to take the time to listen to, hear, and respond to ideas offered by local communities, and a company's failure to establish institutional systems by which two-way communication can regularly and consistently occur with communities, both signal that the ideas of people are of no interest or concern to the company. The outside (company) agenda will dominate local decisions. Local insights and analyses are not valued or respected.

Getting it right with behavior

Getting it right involves respect, trust, and caring

When respect, trust, and caring are demonstrated by the behaviors of company staff and through institutional arrangements, communities speak highly of the company. People point out that there is no way to fake these attitudes. People *know*, they say, if they are respected, or not. They *know* when they are trusted and when they are not. And people say that, within a very short time, they can sense if a company really cares about its impacts on their lives, or if it is just paying lip service to these concerns to protect the company's reputation internationally.

In one community, people told CEP that they appreciated the style of the company staff who always seemed friendly. We did not immediately understand because we knew that company personnel were always busy, moving from place to place on fixed schedules in company cars, and that they were required always to be back in the company compound before dark. How could they appear friendly? As we questioned this, people told us that the company cars were always driven slowly, and this made it possible for them to see who was in the car, wave to them, greet and be greeted by them. They interpreted this as showing that the company cared about the community.

Communities tell us that, for them, respect is a reciprocal concept. If the company demonstrates respect, it can expect to be respected in return. A culture of honor often obliges local leaders to protect a company if it has demonstrated respect for the local people (even if its presence has other negative impacts). Conversely, if the company does not show respect, there is no obligation to protect it, and it is acceptable – even honorable – to attack or undermine company operations.

With regard to trust, people are especially sensitive. Company policies and practices that assume goodwill and honesty confirm and reinforce these qualities. According to local communities, policies and practices of transparency are among the strongest signals of trust. Openness – both the fact of openness and the signal from a company that it intends to be open and above board – reassures a community from the beginning that it will be aware of plans and problems that may affect it. In this way, transparency establishes a relationship that is based in trust, honesty, and forthrightness.

Finally, with regard to caring, as we have noted several times, most communities welcome companies and want them to become active in their area. However, they also want early and regular reassurances that the company that has so much power over their resources and their environment is genuinely concerned about its impacts on the quality of their lives.

Respect, trust, and caring are intangibles and, as such, they appear to be difficult to assess. However, we have learned from community members what they look for to gauge the presence or absence of these intangibles.

What do respect, trust, and caring do for a company? Why are they important?

Give a company a human face

Communities note that everyone wants to be respected and trusted and to see that people who affect their lives really care about them. They see this as simply human. For them, respect, trust, and caring are the values that express common humanity across cultural differences and between companies and communities. They counter worries that the company is a faceless corporate entity concerned only with making a profit.

Set the tone for company–community relationships

Signaling respect, trust, and caring through company policies, practices, and individual staff behavior sets the basic tone for everything else that a company does. As companies enter new communities and unfamiliar cultures, they will make mistakes. When people feel respected, they can approach the person who made the mistake with confidence that they will be listened to and heard. When they feel trusted, they find it easier to trust the other person.

Mitigate risks

Companies have found that when they showed a greater presence in a community this conveyed respect, trust, and caring. Presence also enabled them to dispel rumors and prevent anti-company demonstrations based on their personal relationships with informal leaders and others that helped diffuse tensions.

Respect, trust, and caring about what?

Communities do not want a company to respect things that should not be respected, to trust people who should not be trusted, or to take care of local people (rather than care about them)! As they name these three qualities as fundamental to healthy company–community relationships, they also put very clear limits on them. They do not want a company, and its staff, to be ignorant and easily duped.

In general, communities want companies to be considerate and respectful and trusting in how they deal with people as individuals and as neighbors. Beyond that, companies are also expected to show respect for local social, cultural, and religious norms and values. They do not have to abide by all local norms, but company personnel should acknowledge their importance to local people and convey this acknowledgment.

How can a manager get respect, trust, and caring right?

1. Ask, discuss, and listen

One simple but under-used way to determine how the company and company staff should behave in a new culture is to ask local people what matters to them. A discussion about respectful behavior sends the signal that the company is making an effort to respect local mores, rules, and systems. When staff are observed to honor local customs on a regular basis, the signal of respect is reinforced. A company needs not only to communicate its message *to* communities, but also to develop systems for hearing *from* communities. This is true transparency.

2. Train staff and monitor behavior

Many companies train their international and local staff (who often come from different parts of the country where customs are different) in local context awareness, including cross-cultural communication, as part of their orientation. Some companies hire local elders to provide such training. When word gets around that a company is seriously learning about, and paying for, this kind of knowledge, people feel that this shows respect.

3. Engage openly with communities in decisions that affect their lives

When companies maintain open, regular, and ongoing communication with communities, this signals respect for people's ideas, trust that communities will engage in problem-solving as partners, and caring for how outcomes affect local people's lives. People say that it does not matter whether managers agree with the ideas that communities put forward; they feel more respect from a counterpart who openly and vigorously disagrees with them in honest exchange than they do from a person who always appears to agree but does not follow through.

4. Identify and map culturally significant sites

When companies need to use local land for mining, for roads, or for other aspects of their operations, they should always identify, and honor, the cultural significance of the land they need.

> " We had to construct a road through an area full of sacred objects. With the help of local leaders we identified and mapped trees, rocks, and other objects important to the community. We designed the road to avoid damaging these sacred places. Then we had this big tree. There was no way to design the road without cutting down that tree. So we went to the village to discuss the issue. When we presented our map, they were amazed that we had identified all sacred objects. Then we politely asked the community if there was any way to move the spirit living in that one tree to another tree. Noticing our genuine efforts to minimize our impacts on local culture, the community asked us to give them a few days. The next week they performed a ritual to move the spirit and came back to us to tell us we could cut down the tree. From then on, project implementation went smoothly. "
>
> *(Manager of a construction company)*

5. Present a human face to communities and interact with them

Communities tell CEP that one aspect of establishing neighborly feelings with a newly arrived company has to do with seeing real people. Proximity in physical terms reduces distance in power terms. When managers and other company staff are seen around town, walk comfortably through villages and along streets, sit in cafes and have easy exchange with local people, stop to talk and ask about how things are going, community members are impressed. This is translated as being neighborly (i.e., treating people with respect and trust). The single most important yet simple thing a manager can do to establish initial positive community relations is to take the time to go to representative villages and communities and to sit with people and talk *without appearing to be rushed*. Communities value this more than most managers can imagine because they see the company as made up of real people, and they feel as if these people care about them as real people too.

'Look! The white man has legs!'

One manager sheepishly told the story that, one day, he had a flat tire in the middle of a village that he had driven through countless times on his way to and from the company site. When he stepped out the car to assist the driver to change the wheel he noticed some small kids giggling, while pointing at his legs. When asked, the driver reluctantly translated that the kids were "surprised to see that the white man had legs." The manager realized that he had never set foot in the village and that the children were poking fun at him as they had only seen him chest up through the car window.

---

6. Keep protection and symbols of protection to a minimum

Some companies train their security guards at the compound gate to welcome people and to help visitors find the right people to talk to. Some companies arrange occasional open houses of their compounds for community members. Many ensure that gate guards are unarmed and unthreatening. Arrangements that convey openness and accessibility also communicate trust. Community people say that the wording of documents or the manner in which a negotiation is carried out also reveal whether a company is genuine about providing benefits or is self-protective. These institutional factors buttress the benefits of showing a human face.

7. Use language that people understand

Managers should ensure that major company issues are communicated to local people in languages, and in terminology, they understand. A company representative who avoids overly technical or legalistic language, but instead sits and talks as if to friends, communicates caring and respect. A manager who takes the time to explain technical issues in non-technical ways shows appreciation for the intelligence of local people.

8. Ensure that information is easily accessible to all types and groups of people

This rule has two components: information should be easy to obtain, and everyone should be able to obtain it.

Communities indicate that any of the techniques for establishing transparency (such as public announcements and transparency offices) are useless unless they are frequent, regular, and reliable. Regular reliance on multiple methods always signals readiness to communicate transparently. But a one-time meeting or occasional announcements are viewed with suspicion and are seen to be focused only on getting community approval for some company action rather than as part of a general, ongoing, respectful interaction.

9. Be responsive to community inquiries, questions, and letters

Managers who ensure that every question is answered, promptly and politely, either in meetings or in letters, are seen by communities as respectful and caring. Formalized systems through which communities have easy and safe access to ask questions and receive responses also signal caring. Such mechanisms show that companies and communities can engage around difficult issues in a non-confrontational manner.

10. Follow through on commitments

One of the biggest trust breakers in the relationship between companies and communities is a company's failure to keep promises it has made to communities. To ensure this does not occur, some managers have established a promise or commitment register to document each commitment they make. This register is public and available to community members. Other companies document all occasions where the company keeps its promises to help communities maintain a balanced perspective.

> " We thought that we had not made that many commitments to local communities in our consultation meetings. That was until the IFC went through all our public consultations and disclosure documents. They listed over 150 commitments! That is when we realized that we had to start our commitment register! "
>
> *(General manager of a mining company)*

11. Accept accountability as a right of local communities

Complaints and grievances are inevitable for any type of corporate operation. Establishment of a grievance procedure demonstrates to local communities that a company respects their right to hold it accountable for its behaviors and impacts. A grievance procedure provides one of the most effective tools for dealing with local concerns in a non-violent manner.

Although a grievance by its nature deals with dissatisfaction, the outcome of any complaint will be accepted or rejected based on the transparency of the company's process. Even the best processes and outcomes, when hidden from view, may inflame suspicions.

12. Act, and be seen to act, on requests that go beyond the corporate interest

Communities appreciate a company that assists them in ways that go beyond the direct self-interest of the company. Such gestures can be relatively minor, such as providing a lift to a sick community member on the company plane or, more significant, such as speaking with the government on the community's behalf or providing a venue where government and community representatives can meet. When people say, "the company did not have to do this but chose to," they perceive this as a genuine demonstration of caring.

Conclusion

Managers may find the issues embedded in respect, trust, and caring difficult to understand because of their cultural dimensions. They recognize that different actions convey different messages in different cultures.

CEP found that communities continually explain these intangibles in straightforward and direct ways. They want to know that, when an agreement is reached, it will be honored. Directness, honesty, appreciation, pleasantries, and listening are universally welcomed and cost nothing.

More important for a manager, behavior skills can be learned and institutionalized in standard operating procedures (SOPs). As company personnel have learned to honor and respect the safety, health, and environment protocols, they can as well learn to live with, and further, the community relations behavior protocols. A manager may inventory staff behaviors and institutional behaviors and, locating weaknesses that convey undermining messages, provide options and procedures that reverse negative messages and convey positive messages. Behaviors can be changed and the positive returns in terms of company–community relations can be significant.

4

Side effects
Getting it wrong and getting it right

The side effects issue

The third category for understanding and analyzing company–community relations has to do with the side effects that come with a company's presence and the degree to which a company does, or does not, take responsibility for the impacts of these side effects on people's lives.

Experience shows that the arrival and operations of companies have many side effects, some positive and some negative. For example, the influx of people who come to an area where a company locates looking for jobs and other income opportunities can disrupt local life, or it can represent new energy and creativity in the area. As we discussed, communities want a company to care about them, and one aspect of caring is, they say, demonstrated by a company's accountability both for its direct impacts (discussed above as benefits distribution and behaviors) *and* for its indirect impacts through unintended and/or long-term side effects.

Increasingly, even remote communities are aware that a company's arrival can bring problems as well as benefits. News travels and advocacy groups abound. Even as communities are generally positive about a company's locating in their area, they are also wary about the long-term impacts of the company's presence.

Communities observe whether or not a company acknowledges its indirect impacts and takes responsibility for the way these affect people's lives. It is this — the signals sent by the company's attitude toward its responsibility for indirect impacts — that affects company–community relations.

Getting it wrong with side effects

Experience shows that there are three specific types of negative side effect that often worsen company–community relations.

Influx of outsiders

A company opens operations in a poor society. Inevitably, people from other parts of the country move to the area in order to find jobs. The influx of such outsiders to a small community has a number of negative impacts.

The arrival of many outsiders threatens social cohesiveness as people with differing backgrounds, norms, and modes of doing things enter the area and interact with local people. Further, increasing numbers of people strain existing resources. Environmental damage often results from the sheer number of people crowded into a previously thinly populated area. Disease may follow, for example, when water sources are strained.

Increased demand for goods may cause prices to rise. Because of the new employment opportunities with the company, local farmers or fishermen may find they have to pay increased wages to attract seasonal labor. Although some people always benefit from increased demand for the things they sell, most people say that they suffer from rising prices for food, housing, and transport. Increasing numbers of people also bring extra traffic on the roads, causing more congestion and deterioration of whatever infrastructure exists.

As many of the new arrivals are men (and, often, young men), sexual norms of the receiving community can be challenged. Prostitution may appear; sexually transmitted diseases may increase. The norms of traditional family life often begin to shift in response to such pressures as young women are courted by itinerant youth or by relatively wealthy company employees. Local men complain, "Outsiders are stealing our women." When growing numbers of young men are disappointed in their job seeking (because there are never enough jobs for everyone who comes searching for work), crime may follow.

In these and numerous other ways, disruptive and damaging impacts are common in communities where a company's location causes a population influx. These effects are universally difficult for small communities to handle.

Influx of cash

The second set of negative impacts comes through newly available – and often abundant – cash introduced into the local economy through a company's arrival. When people are compensated for land and crops, when some people gain new monetized jobs, when contracts are let, and when national and expatriate company staff begin to spend on local things, new levels of cash bring new social and political pressures.

In many countries, the influx of new cash results in a challenge to old and traditional leadership. The amount of money a man or woman has becomes a new standard by which people gain importance and power, replacing previous standards of wisdom, age, and experience as prerequisites for political leadership. Often those who are moneyed are also young, and the shift in leadership is reinforced by a rejection of the established ways of doing things and of the older people who formerly were leaders.

In some countries, men with new wealth from a company's payments have taken additional wives either formally or informally. This again puts pressures on traditional family life and kinship relations. Especially in areas where women lose access to their farm lands as a result of corporate operations (a frequent occurrence in Africa) and men move into paid jobs, the impact is to upset traditional gender roles. The negative impacts on women's lives are often disproportional to those on men's lives.

In societies where extended families have traditions of sharing, new cash wealth can be disruptive. Communities describe how traditional systems of sharing have been eroded when one or two family members receive large cash payments from, for example, a company compensation program. The mutuality of kinship expectations and obligations is lost, and greed soon replaces generosity. This tendency is especially reinforced when wealth also translates into power.

The negative side effects from cash are a particular puzzle for local communities who expected that their increasing wealth from a company's operations would bring greater, not less, security and greater, not less, happiness.

Environmental impacts

Communities around the world, from the Sahara to the highlands in Papua New Guinea, are concerned about corporate environmental impacts. They worry about corporate effects on the fertility of their land, the availability and quality of their water, the dust and noise levels they are exposed to, and the quality of air they breathe.

In many societies, people's connections to their land or water, their hills and their forests go far beyond these as factors of production (see Chapter 7 for a fuller discussion of this). Environmental assets represent ties to ancestors, history, a way of life, spiritual meanings, and so on. As a result, concerns over environmental impacts, and especially a perceived lack of company respect for the cultural/religious value assigned to nature, can become particularly troubling.

As a result, managers and community people may speak very different languages as they discuss protection of, and compensation for, natural resources. When a company is unaware of, or ignores, these aspects of people's attachment to nature, issues surrounding the company's environmental impacts can result in company–community conflicts that have lasting political and social, as well as geographical and economic, impacts.

We wish we had known . . .

The profound impact of two of the areas of side effects — influx of people and influx of cash — are seldom anticipated by local communities. Likewise, corporate managers seldom raise these with local communities as they begin their operations because many simply feel that these issues are a natural aspect of progress and change, and that people should know about these issues and figure out how to handle them. They feel that as a company they bear no direct responsibility for these things they cannot control.

However, as the unexpected negative impacts of people and cash influxes unfold and build on each other, communities may become desperately resentful. They experience a range of ways in which the quality of their lives declines even as they expected things to get better. Many communities report that they "wish we had known so we could prepare better."

The third area of negative side effects — environmental impacts — is usually anticipated by communities and companies. However, probable differences in company and community approaches to the natural world, unless acknowledged and dealt with, mean that what could become an area of company–community cooperation around a common concern instead becomes a contentious focus for deteriorating relations.

Getting it right with side effects

When a company acknowledges that its operations will have both immediate and long-term unintended side effects, some of which will be negative, and the company makes clear that it takes responsibility for the impacts of these side effects, it is defining its sphere of accountability broadly. When a community can see that a company is concerned by, and accepts responsibility for, the unintended and long-term side effects of its operations, people interpret this as a sign that the company cares about them and their lives — not just about the company's reputation.

It is apparently difficult to find examples of companies that have handled their long-term side effects well. One journalist told us how he had conducted months of research to write a feature for a respected monthly journal about companies that leave a good legacy in the communities where they work. As he did his research and spoke with dozens of experts, he was consistently referred back to the example of one company. This was the single positive example he found, cited by everyone, although there are thousands of companies of the type he was researching.

Similarly, although CEP has seen some impressive examples of companies taking initiatives to inform communities about likely side effects, and to work with them to prepare for these, strong positive examples are rare.

To support positive company–community relations, therefore, companies need to demonstrate that they are "different." They take responsibility for broader changes in the quality of life of communities during the lifespan of a project and beyond.

What does accountability for side effects do for a company? Why is it important?

Eases all company–community interactions

A community's expectations regarding a company's commitment to broad and long-term positive impacts will affect how that community interacts with the company from day one. Acceptance of accountability for whatever emerges builds a sense of confidence and trust that the company will not let people suffer if something unexpected arises.

Relieves pressure for immediate benefits

Communities that feel that a company is attentive to all of its impacts — intended and unintended, immediate and long-term — do not feel pressure to push aggressively for unreasonable immediate benefits.

Improves a company's international reputation

When a company is seen to care about its impacts in one area, this information shapes its public image. Other countries and other communities are comfortable welcoming the company into their area if it is known to be responsible in this way.

Underlies a more effective, efficient, and strategic community engagement approach

When a company accepts responsibility for its long-term impacts at the outset of a project, it can develop a strategy for company–community involvement that is phased and intentional. This avoids two often observed pitfalls — on the one hand, ad hoc, reactive programming as events (often crises) unfold and, on the other hand, the collapse of company-sponsored benefits (such as schools and clinics) when the project is complete. Designing an approach that takes a long-term perspective helps a company define what it wants to achieve and how it may achieve it, and communicate with communities what it considers to be the boundaries of its responsibilities.

Ensures appropriate budgeting for community programs

When management has a plan and a strategy that relates to the long term, it is able to approve budgets that are based on a well-thought-out approach, rather than face yearly negotiations demanding more money where there is no justification. Companies that have an agreed-upon strategy with communities face much (much!) less pressure from local groups to engage in yearly negotiations over memoranda of understanding. We have seen that, in such cases, the company–community relationship is characterized by engagement and brainstorming rather than by negotiations and demands.

Accountability for side effects: what matters to communities?

In the discussions of the other two categories of corporate–community relations, we have answered the question about what matters to communities with assurance (quoted from communities themselves). Communities have remarkably focused and reasonable expectations in relation to benefits distribution and behavior and their impacts. However, with regard to unintended and future impacts, there is not such clarity. The goals people express are broader and stated in general principles more than in defined actions. For example, people note that they really care, very much, about how a company's presence will affect their quality of life, over the long term. They care about whether, when the company leaves, they will be better off or worse off. They note that their judgments on this issue shape their responses on many of the smaller, more immediate issues that come up during a project.

More specifically, people want to be sure that environmental damage will not leave them without the future resources they need for survival, that their social and political systems will not be destroyed or made less humane by the company's influence, and that they will be economically better off, with a brighter future, than they would have been without the company's presence. They expect the company to improve their lives in many ways.

How can a manager get side effects right?

1. Support people in strengthening their own impact preparedness plan

An important aspect of maintaining local goodwill is to help local communities prepare themselves for changes (such as increased prices, prostitution, or crime rates) that come when a company locates in their area. Increasingly companies are aware that they should inform communities about potential negative side effects from the beginning and work with communities to develop solid plans for addressing these.

2. Have an influx management plan

A company should always anticipate and plan for influx side effects. These are no longer surprising and unexpected for any international company that has had previous projects in poor or troubled countries. An influx management plan should review company policies that attract people to the site (e.g. hiring people at the company gate) and adapt them to avoid attracting excessive numbers of people to the site. It should also focus on mitigating the impact of jobseekers on the host community and include both an infrastructure component and a psychological one. A company can help ensure that there is sufficient water, housing, and transport to handle newcomers, and it can develop programs and support discussions that help communities anticipate and prepare mentally for the changes they will experience from the influx of outsiders and money.

3. Integrate community issues in the project design

Many important decisions that affect communities are made at the desks of engineering companies, located far away from the corporate site and focused on technical issues, especially in the construction phase of a project. When many decisions are being made outside communities, some (but very few) companies have taken steps to ensure that all relevant design aspects are reviewed through a community perspective.

Thinking beyond the project

One manager ordered a generator with a much larger capacity than was needed to run the operation. He explained that the spare capacity allowed him to develop a community-based electricity scheme that accustomed villagers to paying a market rate for electricity. Over time, he felt this would allow the community to buy and maintain its own generator. Another company, working in a socially troubled area where many youngsters were addicted to gas sniffing, developed a type of kerosene to replace gas, to the delight of traditional elders.

---

4. Discuss a long-term vision with communities

Experience shows that development of a shared company–community vision can have positive long-term impacts on local communities. This is because the process of determining a vision forces both companies and communities to state explicitly their definitions of long-term success and the principles by which they will work together to achieve shared goals.

When companies ask communities, "What do you hope your community will look like in 20 years and how will you manage to achieve this?" this encourages the community to determine its own future instead of expecting the company to have all the answers. When medium- and long-term goals and objectives are defined and agreed upon, it becomes possible to develop a strategy and a budget to reach these objectives. An agreed-to plan also serves as a useful tool for both company and community to measure progress.

5. Listen to local communities' concerns regarding side effects

The most direct way to learn of unexpected side effects is to ask local people what they are experiencing. In addition, establishing a system can formalize communities' right to raise side effects issues and to suggest ways of dealing with negative side effects.

6. Provide long-term contracts and training plans

One effective way for a company to demonstrate its commitment to long-term benefits and a broad improvement in people's quality of life is by setting long-term volume targets for employment and contracting . A company can announce its intention to fill a certain percentage of its managerial positions or skilled employee slots from local communities by a certain year and, then, support training programs that ensure that people have the qualifications to fill these jobs.

7. Provide support to existing organizations and existing plans

Supporting existing groups, rather than developing company programs to perform the same functions, is one approach to ensure that company impacts are positive even after a project closes. By recognizing and working through existing community structures, a company reinforces and strengthens these local capacities. Recognizing this, some companies conduct an institutional survey to map the existing expertise of NGOs, government agencies, civil society, and other groups with whom the company can partner.

8. Mitigate the impacts of sudden and large amounts of cash in society

Managers, knowing that large amounts of cash flooding into a society as a result of a company's presence can have negative impacts on the political and social fabric of communities, should discuss this with communities. They could develop approaches for mitigating these impacts and, possibly, provide money-management training, investment advice, and support for the creation of new small business opportunities to help local people avoid or reduce such negative impacts.

The importance of perceptions

Community perceptions are realities for companies. This is true even when perceptions are based on falsehoods or misunderstandings in the eyes of a company manager. When communities say they *feel* disrespected, company managers might attempt to dispute this, arguing that they really do respect the community. Or, they may explain to them why the actions they perceive as disrespectful really do not reflect a negative attitude. Communities are seldom persuaded by explanations or arguments.

Community perceptions are realities for companies

But communities are not dumb. Experience shows that they respond both to what companies do and to how they do it. Doing the right things in the wrong way gains little. Doing the wrong things in the right way also does not work. To change perceptions, a company must first change itself.

The only way to manage community perceptions is through effective management of company attitudes and actions.

Company actions undertaken in each of the three categories described — benefits distribution, behavior, and side effects — grow out of company-held assumptions about communities. In the pages that follow, as we describe the field-based evidence of how companies shape community perceptions, we will also look behind the policies and practices that drive perceptions, identifying the assumptions and attitudes that underlie the what and how of company actions.

A manager who is aware of the linkages by which assumptions flow into practice that shapes perceptions that determine community attitudes is a manager who can create positive company–community relations.

5

Making the transition from getting it wrong to getting it right

What a company should or should not do looks simple when you describe how things can go wrong or right. So why do so many companies run into difficulties? How can they make the transition from **getting it wrong** to **getting it right**?

During visits to various company sites, we kept running into examples of corporate decisions and policies that seemed misguided from an outside perspective. In many situations corporate approaches appeared to make establishing and maintaining cordial relationships with local communities unnecessarily difficult. Community members described the overall impact of corporate presence in negative terms and mostly complained about companies. Company staff said that the communities they worked with were "difficult" and "obstructive."

We also observed that companies that worked in the same countries, in the same contexts, with the same types of stakeholder and authority, and in the same sectors of industry, made decisions that allowed for the development of positive and engaging relationships with local communities. Community members described the overall impact of the corporate presence as positive; company staff felt that communities took a constructive approach and were pleasant (although challenging!) to work with.

It made us wonder why different companies working towards the same objective — establishing positive relations with communities — had such different outcomes and impacts for their efforts. In comparing company approaches, we traced the varying degrees of success between companies back to their corporate policies and practices.

Why do companies operating in the same area use such distinctly different policies and approaches with regard to community relations? After all, the approaches taken by some companies were clearly more successful — according to both the company and the community — than the approaches taken by others.

When we discussed the ideas behind certain policies and approaches with regard to day-to-day aspects of operation with company staff, it became clear that these were driven by the assumptions and mind-sets prevalent in the companies. This observation initially felt very obvious and overly simplistic. There is nothing new in saying that our implicit assumptions and perceptions drive our behavior and approaches, and these approaches determine our level of success (see Fig. 5.1).

Figure 5.1 **How assumptions determine impacts**

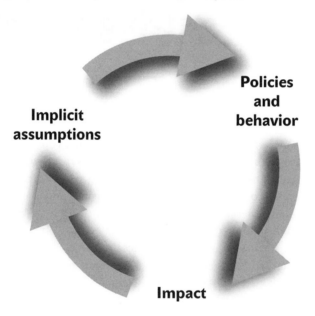

When we started to track relationships between corporate impacts, corporate policies/practices, and the implicit assumptions on which these were based, we observed discernible patterns. These can best be illustrated by an example we encountered in one particular country. In that country, two oil companies operated in the same region and under similar conditions. Both companies aimed to mitigate social risks to their staff and assets, but with very different approaches.

The first company assumed that, from a risk mitigation perspective, local communities were a risk to the company. This implicit assumption meant that the company provided little information to the communities because they thought the information could be used against the company. The company also minimized contact with the "risk." It engaged with the communities only when there was a need: a crisis or an urgent demand. After all, company staff were discouraged from engaging with risks by their colleagues from the security department. When staff engaged with the communities, their security colleagues would be sure to accompany them.

The result of this approach was predictable: the crisis-response mode conveyed a short-term approach, reinforcing the communities' determination to push for immediate benefits rather than engage in long-range planning and cooperation. In addition, lack of contact meant there was no basis for anticipating or solving problems; limited information sharing led to rumors and disinformation about the company. Youth – and others – were genuinely insulted by the company's use of security providers during community visits and said, "If the company sees us as a risk, we will make sure we will become one." No matter how much money the company invested in community projects, the relationship with the communities did not improve.

From the same risk mitigation perspective, the second company assumed that local communities should be considered partners. It made a point of proactively engaging with the communities on an ongoing basis. Such interactions allowed the company to provide information about its policies and practices, solicit suggestions from community leaders about the types of approach the company should take and, most importantly, build relationships with community members. Based on a long-term strategy developed with communities, the company made efforts to ensure that local youth had access to vocational training and increased job opportunities.

The results were equally predictable: the communities started to see the company as a catalyst for a better future. When community leaders had requests or concerns, they discussed these first with company representatives. Occasionally, company staff would be warned by their friends in the communities about rumors of rebel groups in the area and were advised to avoid certain insecure areas. Because the company defined success in terms other than only avoiding the negative, it ensured that the communities served as a "security cordon," in the words of the security manager. The company also capitalized on opportunities to have positive social impacts.

When we discussed our observations with the staff of the first company, it shocked them to see that their own assumptions informed policies that had the opposite impact from what they had hoped to achieve. Because their assumptions were so subtle and implicit, none of the company staff had been aware of their importance until they were made explicit.

Over the course of the CEP, we have observed many instances where a breakdown in the relationship between companies and communities could be traced

Table 5.1 **Impacts of some underlying corporate assumptions**

Assumption	Policy or practice	Risk or impact
Every problem has a monetary solution	Compensation for damaging livelihoods, spills, or accidents, rather than addressing root causes (cleaning up a spill, restoring an area after mine closure, etc.)	A focus on monetary solutions undermines the perceived need by the company to establish a genuine relationship. Many things important to people have no monetary value. People get upset when they perceive the company thinks it can buy them off
If it is legal, it is justified	Referring people to legal channels to address issues of concern; reliance on security forces	The company is seen as arrogant. If legal redress is beyond reach, communities feel they have no option but to use force to support their claims
Social investment (SI) projects are the best tool to address company–community conflict	Low attention to how operational day-to-day policies impact communities	The company does not check whether a project is the right approach to address the problem. The same problems keep coming back and even increase. Jealousy over SI projects can exacerbate conflict between groups
The community is interested only in immediate and tangible gains	Focus on short-term projects (e.g., buildings), rather than ongoing relationships	Communities do not take ownership of projects (they never asked for them). Company accused of not caring and throwing useless projects at them
More contact and information-sharing will lead to more demands	Engagement only when needed	Communities get attention only when there is a problem; obstructive behavior is rewarded
Community relations (CR) is not one of the core operational activities and core operational activities do not affect CR	Absence of CR from the project design, lack of investment in staff professionalization and no integration of CR in the reward structure	Companies take a reactive rather than preventive approach. Silo mentality means no ownership for CR within the organization. Message to the community is that anything goes as long as production targets are reached

back to underlying corporate assumptions. Some of the prevalent assumptions are shown in Table 5.1.

Obviously, this is not an exhaustive list of corporate assumptions. Nor do we see all of them in all companies. We list them here merely to point out that *all* corporate policies and practices are based on certain assumptions. Making these assumptions explicit helps identify the reasons that corporate policies and practices go right or go wrong. Once managers' eyes are open to the relationship between their assumptions and their policies, they realize that they have many more options to influence the quality of relationships between the company and local stakeholders than they thought.

Linking impacts to corporate policies and practices that are driven by corporate assumptions completes the CEP framework that we introduced in Chapter 1.

In the remaining chapters in this book, we will highlight many of these underlying assumptions in further detail. It is important to remember that making these assumptions explicit helps to clarify why some aspects of company–community relations go poorly and that it is possible to transform these negative aspects by taking the steps shown in Figure 5.2 and expanded below. See the italicized example after each step.

Step 1: Identify the negative impacts observed as a result of the company's presence

> *Conflict between local people and outsiders that are hired by the company for jobs that local people say they can do*

Step 2: Identify the causes of impact and policies or practices they are related to

> *Perceived unfairness. Because the selection criteria for recruitment are solely based on merit, outsiders with a better education are preferred by the company. Local people feel they host the company and should get benefits (such as jobs) to compensate for the negative impacts as a result of the corporate arrival*

Step 3: What is the underlying assumption that led to the implementation of this policy or practice?

> *The assumption is that, in a context of historic differences and conflict, the only way to stay "neutral" as a company is to hire strictly based on merit*

Step 4: Reverse or adapt the assumption

> *An adaptation would be to assume that local people have their own definition of fairness, as well as their own definition of local, and that hiring based on merit is not a neutral approach*

Step 5: Review policies and practices based on the adapted assumption

> *Discuss definition of what it means to be local and determine a protocol that provides benefits to local people, as well as satisfies the corporate need for qualified people.*

Figure 5.2 **Steps to transform negative aspects of company–community relations**

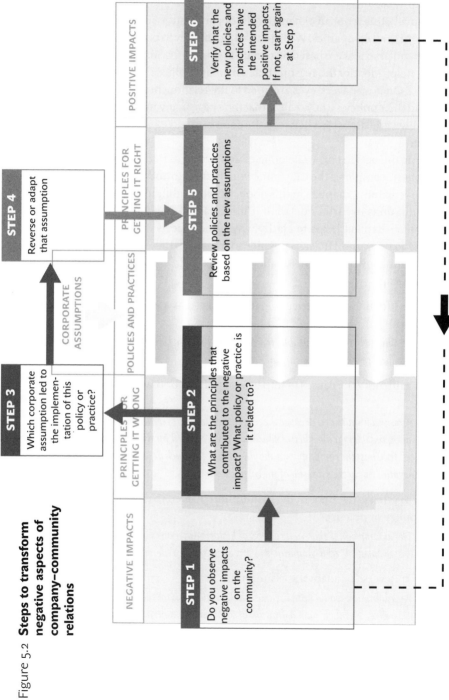

Providing transparency on job qualifications while agreeing that local people who meet these criteria get preference might increase the acceptance of outsiders who are hired for positions that cannot be filled by local people

Step 6: Verify whether the adapted policies and practices have the intended positive impact

Better relations between local people and "outside" employees.

If there is no change in the original observed negative impact, or if the negative impact worsens, go back to Step 1 and try to determine what other policies, practices, and assumptions are undermining company–community relations

Special note on corporate operations in situations of conflict

" In the oil business, all the safe places have been taken. If we are going to find new sources, we have to be willing to go to countries where there is violence. "

(Oil executive)

Many corporations, particularly those that are involved in the extraction of natural resources, find themselves operating in areas of instability and violence. Few corporate managers have any training in conflict resolution or any experience of how to function productively in a violent context. Operations managers frequently say they feel powerless in relation to surrounding instability or violence. They see it as existing before they arrived and beyond their control. As a result, they focus only on limiting the impacts of violence on their company operations and ensuring security for company staff.

There is a great deal of evidence that company managers have much more control over conflict and violence than they believe. This is true even in societies where violence predates the company's arrival. The fact that managers have a much greater level of control over their environment is a recurring theme in this book. As we discussed in the chapters on benefit distribution, behavior, and side effects, company processes can be designed and implemented in ways that can create, exacerbate, or prolong tension and violence among local communities or in ways that can mitigate and reduce tendencies toward violence. This means that managers are not powerless in these contexts. They can have positive effects on a context of conflict without becoming experts in conflict resolution!

To understand how to exert the power they have to mitigate conflict, it is important for company managers to understand and differentiate among the levels of conflict they may encounter in their operating environment. This note provides a guide to these levels and suggests options, derived from experience, that managers have for dealing with each level.

The different levels of conflict affecting companies

There are essentially four different situations that confront company managers: wars and insurrections; company becoming a proxy target for community grievances against the government; inter-communal tensions; and company–community conflict.

Wars or insurrections involve armies, militias, or rebel groups whose operations interact with company work. Such conflicts are related to the wider socio-political context and are not linked to the corporate presence. The causes of wider macro-level conflicts can be diverse and often include basic and long-standing issues such as poverty, social, and political marginalization, injustice, opportunism, greed, and power struggles among powerful people. There are no quick fixes for these conflicts, and a company neither can nor should try to address them on its own. However, companies are not totally powerless even in these situations.

Although each context of conflict is different and it is difficult to generalize, evidence across various contexts teaches us that warring parties often find it more difficult to target a company that has broad support from local communities for its activities, and easier to target a company that has limited local support. This is particularly true when factions are dependent on local communities for resources such as food, shelter, information, and recruits to sustain their struggle.

CEP has worked in communities where rebel groups and/or communities have told us that so long as "the people" like the company and see its benefits in their lives, the armed groups will not target company personnel or property. However, when companies are seen to be mistreating local people, they become open targets for insurrectionist groups. Good company–community relations, therefore, provide a possible, albeit imperfect, safeguard from the violence of war.

Corporations can become the proxy targets for community grievances against their government. These grievances typically center on the national government's failure to provide social services or the lack of revenue flows back to communities where resources are being extracted. When local communities see that they are not benefiting from the corporate presence but government leaders are using revenues generated by companies for personal gain, to purchase arms, or sometimes even to suppress local discontent, they take out their resentments against their government on the nearby operations of the company. For marginalized communities, sabotaging company assets can be seen as their best or only option to attract government attention to obtain public services or, on a grander scale, justice.

Getting the government's attention

In Papua New Guinea, one community in a remote location chopped down a power line essential to mining operations. The community later apologized to the company, leaving a note near the power line stating that its actions were not against the company, but were intended to attract the attention of the government. It worked and the action led to joint efforts between the government and the company to address local grievances. The community now has its own police post and a new school.

A company can be aware of the failures of government to address local problems and take steps to address the distance between government and people. Some companies have created venues and opportunities for local communities to meet with government officials for discussions. Some have developed tripartite arrangements for addressing local needs that include government. Any company actions that prevent misuse of company resources by corrupt government officials will, at the same time, reduce the likelihood that the company will be a proxy target for government inaction or injustice.

Intergroup or inter-communal tensions in a company's area of operations are also important influences on corporate operations. Even when a company is an outsider to pre-existing and ongoing local conflicts among groups, its day-to-day business operations are considered by those involved in the conflict as important to and having an impact on the outcome of their struggles. Such broader societal conflicts must be considered by corporate managers because these tensions may be inadvertently exacerbated by corporate operations. A deterioration of relations among local adversaries frequently backfires on a corporation. In other chapters, we have shown how the distribution of company benefits may inadvertently reinforce and exacerbate pre-existing intergroup divisions, and we have suggested ways that company managers may design their operations to support and build on aspects of communities' lives that cross such divisions and connect people. Companies have a great deal of control over their impacts on these community "dividers" and "connectors." (See Chapter 2 and all chapters in Section II.)

Company–community conflict is the most visible to managers because its impacts reach the company immediately in the form of complaints, demands, threats, or obstructive activities. As we have noted in previous chapters, companies can make it difficult for local communities to get attention without acting in violent or obstructive ways when they do not respond to requests or complaints in a timely way. When companies do not respond to quiet complaints but immediately respond to sabotage or shutdowns, this can inadvertently encourage and reward violence (see Chapter 2 on benefits distribution).

Clearly managers have a great deal of control over company–community conflict. Conflict of this sort should never be considered "outside the control" of the company.

The level of control that a company manager can exert over these four levels of conflict varies. Managers have limited, but still some, control over violence they may experience from warfare but have increasing control over whether they become proxy targets, whether they exacerbate intergroup conflict or support intergroup connectors, and whether they enjoy positive or suffer from negative interactions with the communities.

Figure 5.3 depicts these direct and indirect relationships, showing that companies always operate within a context and, therefore, interact with it. Companies have immediate and direct interactions with their surrounding communities. These communities, in turn, have sometimes positive and sometimes negative

Figure 5.3 **The wider context of conflict**

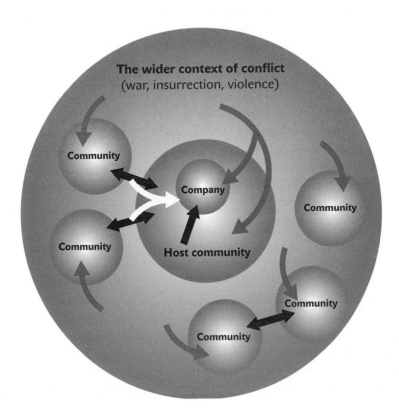

interactions with other communities and, depending in part on company actions, these inter-community relations can bounce back as violence against the company. All communities – and the company – exist in the broader social and political context, and their interactions at this level with government, rebel groups, and others, as described above, can bring that broader context back into company–community relations – often in the form of violence against the company. Even here, as the arrows in Figure 5.3 show, company actions can make some difference as to whether or not these broader problems also become problems for a company.

Proxy conflict also becomes company–community conflict

The different levels of conflict are often dynamic and can overlap. What starts as one type can adopt the characteristics of another over time. For example, the conflict in the Niger Delta originated with disputes between local communities and the central government over the share of oil revenues being returned to the communities. Increasingly, oil companies were used as proxy targets by local communities to express grievances to the faraway, otherwise unreachable, government in Abuja. Over time the conflict changed. Local communities positioned themselves against oil companies operating in the Niger Delta region, accusing them of inadequately compensating communities for oil spills, using government police forces known for their poor human rights records, and not sufficiently asserting their political leverage with the government to increase the quality of life of local communities. In response, the oil companies say that they have been instrumental in assuring that 13% of the oil revenues in Nigeria now flow from the federal level to the oil-producing states. But by the time the companies addressed the proxy issue of revenue flows this did not result in a reduction of violence and tension because the conflict had changed. The companies have not yet addressed the grievances communities are holding against them.

Conflict is predictable and preventable

Regardless of the level, conflict it is usually predictable. People around the world have similar needs and expectations and they become disappointed over similar issues. Local communities across the world react in similar ways when they perceive that a company does not respect them or benefit their lives. Because local community happiness is a company's best buffer from conflict, whether because the community protects company assets from rebel attack or because the community finds it advantageous to work with rather than against a company, it is always important to keep close to and aware of community reactions to company operations.

If conflict does not come out of the blue, then what are the signals that managers could watch out for that would indicate there is an increasing risk of violence?

Conflict toward a company typically erupts after an incident or event. These can be relatively minor events (including those under the control of the company such as late payments to employees or contractors) which trigger an underlying frustration. Larger incidents, such as environmental accidents, can also be triggers when these directly affect people's day-to-day lives and are not adequately addressed. Other triggers may occur outside the control of a company, such as a government raid on a rebel group in the area, but may still unleash a level of violence that involves the company if there is disgruntlement toward the company among local groups.

A manager who is aware of how triggers work will be alert to signals of tension between the company and the community. Possible indictors include the presence of groups that have an interest in creating conflict. These can be politicians, NGOs campaigning on an anti-corporate platform, contractors seeking claims due to work interruptions (*force majeure*), or youth groups seeking security contracts who may benefit from keeping the situation insecure in order to demonstrate that their services are needed. Managers should also watch for groups of people complaining and hanging around the company gates. Often, unemployed people milling about waiting for jobs have little to lose, and their frustration can easily be manipulated by outsiders.

One reliable indictor is the proportionality of community reaction to relatively minor incidents. For example, if a company car kills a goat and this leads to a large and angry demonstration at the company gates, this probably signals a lot of dissatisfaction about other issues.

As we will discuss in Chapter 14 on key indicators, being alert to changes in community behavior and responses can help managers see misunderstandings and frustrations in an early stage when there is time to prevent violence.

Conflict might be preventable but where to start addressing it?

The first step in prevention is to eliminate company-prompted incentives for local groups to behave violently and to create mechanisms to address disagreements constructively, respectfully, and transparently. Next, a manager should review how all operational activities increase or decrease the likelihood for conflict. The details of these influences are covered in Section II of this book.

The **conflict lens** in Figure 5.4 provides an overview of how all operational decisions (hiring, compensation, security, etc.) can be assessed for their likely influ-

Figure 5.4 **Conflict lens**

Key: P peace; C conflict

DECISIONS ABOUT OPERATIONS

COMPENSATION   HIRING   CONTRACTING   SECURITY
GOVERNMENT RELATIONS   COMMUNITY CONSULTATION
COMMUNITY PROJECTS   RELOCATION

---

1. **Do company operations reward destructive (not necessarily violent) or constructive behavior?**
   - Do more peaceful communities get more benefits (P) than difficult ones (C)?
   - Is there a more immediate response to letters/complaints (P) or to threats/closedowns (C)?
   - Are communities visited informally (P) or only when there is a need (C)?

2. **Do company operations convey disrespect or respect for stakeholders?**
   - Do communities perceive that all promises are followed through (P) or not (C)?
   - Do stakeholders know about long-term corporate benefits (P) or do they feel they benefit more from a short-term approach based on conflict (C)?
   - Are communities involved in decisions that affect their lives (P) or not (C)?
   - Are grievances handled through dialogue (P) or with security backup (C)?
   - Is there transparency about company policies and practices (P) or not (C)?

3. **Do company operations increase or decrease people's security and quality of life?**
   - **Economic:** positive (P) or negative (C) impact on livelihoods?
   - **Political:** increased (P) or decreased (C) influence over leadership?
   - **Environmental:** decreased (P) or increased (C) pollution? Increased (P) or decreased (C) availability of scarce resources?
   - **Physical:** increased safety (P) or increased criminality or insecurity (C)?
   - **Social, cultural, psychological:** increased (P) or decreased (C) capacity of local people to deal with changing norms and values?

4. **Do company operations contribute to intergroup fragmentation or cohesion?**
   - Are benefits distributed in an inclusive/connecting (P) way or an exclusive/dividing (C) way?
   - Is the hiring policy fair (P) or does it favor (C) certain groups?
   - Do the representatives that the company deals with enjoy popular support (P) or not (C)?
   - Do all landowners/users get the same level of compensation (P) or do more vocal or powerful ones get more (C)?

5. **Do the company operations increase or decrease the capacity/willingness of authorities to provide services?**
   - Does the company effectively lobby to have social services provided (P) or does it substitute for government services (C)?

6. **Do company operations increase or decrease the capacity of authorities to commit violence?**
   - Do authorities use revenues for civil purposes (P) or for warfare (C)?
   - Does the company abstain from (materially) supporting one party to the conflict (P) or not (C)?

Do any operational decisions increase conflict?
If yes, re-examine decisions and redesign policies and programs

ences on violence through six questions, which evidence shows are of great importance. In the conflict lens, the import of these six questions is illustrated by examples that can either increase the likelihood of conflict (C) or the likelihood of stability/peace (P).

Although most companies do not operate in a context of warfare or rebel insurrection, most managers nonetheless encounter one or another level of conflict as described here. For most managers, understanding how their own company operations interact with local communities is the essential conflict lens required to implement day-to-day activities without heightening the likelihood of community anger – and violence – toward the company.

SECTION II

6

Hiring policies

Ahmed's task was to establish a corporate office in a new country to start exploration activities. Because this was an area of high unemployment, he anticipated that local communities would have unrealistically high expectations about employment. He was also aware that there were ethnic conflicts in the area that sometimes erupted into violence. To avoid accusations of favoritism, he decided that the way to show his neutrality was to hire solely based on merit. However, his efforts to be fair were not appreciated by local communities who accused the company of favoring "outsiders" over local people. Rumors about upcoming protests started to reach the managing director's office.

The hiring issue

Company-generated employment provides an important opportunity for average citizens, particularly youth or others without land, to benefit from a company's presence and gain legitimate access to cash. Jobs are one of the biggest corporate contributions to a local economy and should, theoretically, solidify company–community relations. However, in place after place, issues surrounding jobs become a major source of tension.

What goes wrong?

Conflict may arise over employment opportunities for locals and for outsiders

Companies commit themselves to hiring locally. Almost all define local according to some geographical boundary that seems reasonable. Sometimes local is meant to refer to people from the nation where work is done. In other situations, companies refer to a specific area that is directly impacted by, or adjacent to, corporate activities as local.

Communities define local through a range of lenses. Local may refer to the place of birth, to ancestry, to current residence, and so on.

When company and community are working from different ideas of what it means to be local, they may talk past each other as they try to discuss employment issues. A company may be trying its best to respond to community concerns about local hiring while communities may be blocking the company gate accusing the company of unfairly hiring outsiders.

> Companies and communities sometimes have different definitions of "local"

Although most managers would like to give preference to local people, they find that often local people do not meet the company's job qualifications. This is especially true in rural areas where formal education opportunities are low. So the company — and its contractors — are compelled to recruit qualified staff from a wider geographical area. When local communities are under the impression — right or wrong — that the company, or its contractors, brings in outsiders for work they believe can be done by local people, managers can be sure they will encounter protests.

Hiring based on merit can inadvertently reinforce divisions among groups

Companies regularly announce that they are politically neutral with regard to ethnic or other sub-group conflict. They adopt policies that are intended to avoid the perception of bias or favoritism among groups.

However, communities are made up of groups, which often operate according to historical patterns by which some groups are advantaged and others disadvantaged. Systems of exclusion, racism, prejudice, and privilege often underlie intergroup tensions.

One frequently seen result of internal community dynamics is a systematic advantaging of some groups over others in access to education. Companies' criteria for hiring often include education as a sought-after qualification. When education is a factor specified for merit hiring, the hiring outcome can reinforce established historical inequities. What is intended by managers as a neutral policy, in fact reinforces the status quo. This may feed into and exacerbate divisions in that community. And, of course, communities that perceive they are being marginalized often respond negatively to the company.

What was intended as a neutral policy reinforces the status quo and can feed into conflict

" These folks in the company are hypocrites. They say they care about us, the local people. But they employ people from the same elites and tribes that have been in power in this country for decades and have always gotten rich over our backs. And now the same people are sitting in the top floors of the company building. Meanwhile, the oil the company is exploiting is *our* oil. The only 'benefit' we get is to work for $1 per day as security guards! "

(Local security guard at oil site)

Delegating hiring decisions to third parties can lead to bias and backfire on the company

Companies sometimes decide to leave the hiring of local labor to local actors: for example, local community groups, contractors, or governments. They see this as a way to give communities ownership of fair hiring practices.

Leaving hiring decisions to local actors does not guarantee fairness. This is because community groups or local contractors are part of local power divisions. This can lead them to bring employees from other regions whom they have trained and whom they can trust (perhaps because of family ties or clan loyalty). Local communities may not see them as impartial.

" In order to avoid conflict with communities over hiring outsiders, we left it up to the Community Employment Committee to put forward local candidates for non-skilled labor positions. Then we realized that the authority and legitimacy that we provided to the Employment Committees created opportunities for corruption. The price for outsiders to be qualified as 'local' was three chickens. By trying to do the right thing, we effectively increased the potential for bribery of the Committee members as well as reinforced the division between the haves and the have-nots as those that are able to afford a bribe have a better chance of obtaining a job. "

(External affairs director of a construction company)

When companies are in the process of establishing themselves and are not yet fully staffed, they want to avoid what they see as the troubling exercise of hiring staff, so they may rely on intermediaries such as "fixers" or "body shops" to provide them with laborers. These employment agencies provide labor pools for the company by hiring laborers at a fixed rate and making them available for company jobs.

Using body shops creates resentment against the company for allowing exploitative practices to occur

One problem with this approach is that such intermediaries typically pay extremely low wages in order to maximize their own profit margins. A company may not be aware of this or may know that this is the usual practice and, therefore, feel it is acceptable. However, even though local people work for this body shop at the rates offered in other jobs, they may resent the company for allowing, supporting, and benefiting from an unfair exploitative system it could have changed.

In several areas, company managers who hired local employment agencies have told CEP that they were astounded to learn that the agency recruited from groups that came from outside the region where the company worked. Again, they discovered this was a problem only when local communities protested disruptively.

Government interference can lead to discrimination and politicization of hiring

The problem of government interference is more difficult for a company to handle. A government's interest may be in handing out well-paid jobs to its own constituencies or it may fear that a company's resources and influence could support opposition groups. In some contexts, corporate activities generate much-needed revenues for the authorities to finance the conflict to which they are party. These authorities involve themselves in the hiring process because they fear the company will hire members of opposition groups and, in turn, those group members will relay information that could make it easy for their group to attack the company facility, cutting off a revenue source to the authorities.

For their part, communities have little sympathy for the dilemma that companies face when a government has influence in the selection process. They see this approach as evidence of a company's affiliation with the ruling class. This affiliation is perceived as unfair and makes the company a target for anyone who opposes government policies.

Non-transparent hiring policies can turn frustrated job seekers against the company

Companies have unforeseen activities for which they need laborers on short notice. Although managers acknowledge the safety and security risks associated with, sometimes, large groups of unemployed people hanging around the front gates, it is convenient for managers to have a pool of people readily available to work.

Communities often accuse companies of deliberately keeping job seekers in the dark in order to benefit from this cheap and readily available labor. New company sites attract large groups of job seekers, some of whom come long distances. They leave their families and use their savings (or take out loans) to sustain themselves for the time they think it will take to gain employment. They rent cheap rooms (sometimes in exchange for labor) and hang around the company gates in anticipation of vacancies or a response to their job application. Job seekers say that, unless the company explicitly says it no longer has vacancies, they will stay and hope for a job. By the time it is clear that the company is no longer hiring, job seekers may be so frustrated and so much in debt to local businesses that it takes little encouragement for them to get involved in criminal activities (mainly targeting local communities) or to engage in activities against the company.

Sudden retrenchment can lead to company–community tension

Companies inevitably deal with retrenchment — sometimes of large groups — of employees, either their own staff or contractor staff. When a company has a large start-up construction phase before operations begin, many job opportunities come to an end once the construction is complete. Many company managers consider the end of a temporary contract to be simply a business transaction.

Even when communities had repeated warnings from the company that job opportunities were coming to an end, they say they were not prepared for what seemed like the sudden loss of hundreds of jobs. They say they find it hard to adjust to lower income levels, especially after getting used to plenty of money floating around. When the company retrenches without seeming to make any effort to help the affected employees maintain their incomes, community outrage is a real possibility. Sudden retrenchment is seen as especially unfair when communities know that a company is hiring others at the same time, and when the people they hire are from outside, or when new hires have used political connections to get the job.

> •• We are dealing with an employee who is very well connected to local politicians, whom we need to get our expansion plan approved. We have evidence that this guy is involved in corrupt practices, which is known in the community. The issue is that if we fire this person, it may create additional obstacles getting the political support we need. On the other hand, if we continue to employ him, local communities think we are unfair. And, they point out that, if we allow our own staff to cheat even us, it is evidence that the same staff will also cheat the community. ••
>
> *(Managing director of an oil company)*

Options for getting it right

What options do managers have to ensure that their hiring and employment policies do not create or feed into tensions?

Maximize short-term employment opportunities for local people

Communities are generally keenly aware that very few of them can meet the company requirements for skilled or managerial positions. They accept this, provided the company demonstrates that it is making efforts to increase the chances for local people to gain the jobs for which they are qualified. If local people observe that none of them has access to company jobs, and the company takes no responsibility for this, this leads to resentment of the company in the community.

- **Define local.** Agree with local communities on the definition of who should be considered local and who are outsiders.

- **Publicly commit to hiring local community members for all jobs for which they are qualified.** Increasingly, companies adopt a policy to fill 100% of non-skilled positions with local people.

- **Include requirements for local hiring for contractors through contractual clauses.**

- **Take responsibility for hiring all non-skilled labor for contractors.**

- **Maximize the number of people that can benefit from unskilled employment opportunities.** Use manual rather than mechanized labor where possible.

Invest in long-term local employment opportunities

A few companies have developed comprehensive strategies to ensure that local communities can qualify for skilled company jobs in the long term. Efforts to increase education opportunities are too often focused on a few bright students through scholarship schemes. Better strategies would focus on raising education standards across the board to help more local people get access to jobs (either with this company or with other companies).

- **Support the education system.** Provide better housing for teachers as an incentive to keep them in an area or support vocational training centers or refresher training incentives for teachers.

- **Commit to local hiring targets.** Designate a specific percentage of management staff to be hired from surrounding communities within a given number of years. Provide training and/or apprenticeships to ensure this target can be met.

- **Help local people get officially certified for skills they already possess.** One company found many skilled drivers who could not get jobs because they did not have driver licenses. By paying for their driving tests, the company helped many drivers find employment.

Increase the chances for community members, especially youth, to gain employment

Although local communities understand that they generally do not meet job requirements, they do expect the company to make efforts to increase their chances over time.

- **Provide apprenticeships to youth.** This targeted support helps local young people move from non-skilled to skilled positions.

- **Require contractors to hire a trainer to ensure that local employees who have minimal experience acquire required skills.**

- **Include in the requests for tender a requirement that contractors take on apprentices as a ratio (e.g., 5%) of their overall staff.**

- **Establish a partnership with vocational training centers to train local people.** Over time, this allows for more of the workforce to be recruited from the local area.

Adopt hiring policies that address distributional impacts

In countries where certain (ethnic, religious, tribal) groups have had better access to education compared to other groups, companies should ensure that their hiring policies do not reinforce an unjust and inequitable status quo. In all areas, it is important to recognize the distributional impacts of hiring and find ways to relate hiring policies to policies in other areas (such as contracting or community livelihood projects) that distribute benefits more inclusively.

- **Ensure the staff pool represents the diversity of the population to avoid bias and accusations of bias.**

- **Hire groups of people in society that — by community consensus — should benefit from job opportunities based on their social needs (a connector!).** Some companies that work with a mainly female population, such as flower farms, have a policy of supporting the most vulnerable such as single, female heads-of-household and older (for whom it is more difficult to find a job) and disabled women.

- **Help local people take advantage of business opportunities.** For every job created by a company, many jobs are created by contractors or as a result of increased economic activity in the area (hotels, restaurants, suppliers, convenience stores, etc.). Some companies establish business development centers, set up microcredit programs, or serve as guarantors with local banks to help local entrepreneurs get access to cash. These initiatives help businesses and individuals benefit from the economic opportunities that arise from the corporate presence. Linking these to the economy of the broader region and beyond has even more positive impacts.

More than just technical criteria

One mining company uses a two-step selection process. A community relations officer conducts the first selection of staff based on social selection criteria (number of family members to feed, ownership of a house, present earning power, etc.) and this is followed by a technical officer who conducts the second selection based on technical qualifications.

Ensure that retrenchment processes are perceived as respectful and fair

Retrenchment, especially for a large group of people, can negatively affect company–community relations, or it can allow the company to show respect for employees and demonstrate concern for its long-term impacts. Concern for local employees does not necessarily end with the completion of on-site work, for instance, at the end of the construction phase.

- **Communicate about retrenchment with staff and the wider community.** Hold information sessions, answer questions on local radio shows, and give explanations in local newsletters.

- **Have an accredited institution recognize relevant work experience.** Workers should get formal certification for experience they gained with the company, so they can get access to other construction-related jobs. The timing of such accreditation is important. Recognition counters negative sentiments associated with the end of a construction phase and retrenchment.

- **Provide support after retrenchment.** Set up an office to assist retrenched workers in writing a resume and provide language or computer courses. Set up a local workers inventory that can be distributed to other companies to facilitate job searches of former workers. Organize a bi-weekly workers forum where former employees can meet, exchange ideas, express their frustration, and keep up to date about company events.

- **Ensure that lay-offs are evenly spread across communities.** This spreads the pain of retrenchment and avoids perceptions of bias. Another option is to distribute remaining jobs on a rotation basis (rather than employing 100 staff on a full-time basis, employ 200 people on a 50% basis).

Ensure transparency in hiring criteria

Taking a transparent approach is important for avoiding community suspicions that jobs are allocated on the basis of unfair criteria.

- **Use community bulletin boards to advertise vacancies.** This approach is important even where local candidates do not meet the qualifications for the jobs.

- **Clarify the chances for employment.** If people know about their chances of getting a job they can make reasoned decisions about their prospects.

- **Use public lotteries to select candidates for non-skilled labor to ensure fairness and avoid accusations of corruption.**

Knowing that you got it right

No matter how well designed and implemented the hiring policy, it is not possible to satisfy all job seekers. Still, degrees of satisfaction can vary greatly, and it is important for a manager to know if employment is an issue that is leading to broad community dissatisfaction or if local stakeholders are acknowledging company efforts to **get it right**. Following are some indicators that signal the company is on the right track:

- People have no complaints about outsiders taking jobs for which locals say they are qualified.

- People say the distribution of jobs among individuals and communities is accepted as fair.

- People say that the company makes a good effort to help their chances to access a range of jobs, including management positions, in the long run.

- Communities say that training, apprenticeships, and other company efforts provide them with a better basis from which to seek employment with other companies.

- Staff who have been retrenched do not engage in sabotage or protests.

- People do not loiter at the company gate.

All companies are closely watched by local communities to ensure they have a positive hiring strategy. An approach that is seen as fair, inclusive, respectful, transparent, and providing long-term improvement, is an important aspect of establishing durable positive relationships with local communities.

7

Compensation policies

Joe, the site manager for a large mining company, knew he had a challenge when he looked across the countryside. He could see numerous small houses and farming plots spreading in a patchwork quilt across the hillsides where the mining operation would need to be located. He called his legal officer and his community relations officers into his office and charged them with getting agreement on land compensation levels for these farmers. He said, "Go consult with the people to inform them about what the law requires and how we intend to compensate them. Then, get them to agree on a price for their land that falls within the legal requirements. Our Project Department wants this done in time to start construction in six months. You might want to get some of the biggest landowners to agree first. This may create a snowball effect."

The land compensation issue

For mining, oil, gas, logging, and plantation-type agri-businesses, one of the first interactions with communities occurs when a company needs land. Enterprises must gain access to the resource they depend on, and often they also need spaces for supporting infrastructure such as waste dumps, supply roads, or pipelines. Very often, they need *a lot* of land.

And, very often, the space they need is occupied by rural people — farmers with long and traditional ties to the land where they live and work.

Companies want to get land acquisition *right*. They want to compensate local people fairly and follow legal requirements. Still, a company's approach to acquiring land often becomes one of the earliest major issues that strains company–community relations.

> A company's approach to acquiring land becomes one of the earliest major issues that strains company–community relations

What goes wrong?

The company and the community hold different views about land

Companies think of land as one of the factors of production they need to buy. They assume that acquisition of land is a straightforward business transaction.

Rural people often see land as much more than real estate. They value their land for its cultural and historic significance. In many contexts, the relationship between people and their land is so strong that they cannot be divided. Companies will claim they can do what they wish after acquiring land ("a deal is a deal"), but, for many communities, the land will always belong to them. Land is identity.

'What will I do for the rest of my life?'

Scene 1. The manager complains: "We have offered these people much more than their land is worth, and they just keep on demanding more and more! I am going to use the government's standards and forget this negotiation that will never end."

Scene 2. The community relations officer, fearing the outcry that would ensue if his company backtracked to the government guidelines, which were lower than the company had already offered, goes to the village. He asks a farmer, "What's going on here? Why are you asking these unreasonable amounts for your land?" The farmer answers, "Because I am a farmer. If the company takes my land, I don't know what I will do for the rest of my life. The land is my work *and* my life. If the company wants my land, they need to pay me enough to live on for the rest of my life without land."

Many rural people value their land as the home of their ancestors and, if they have buried their ancestors on that land, as the home of their ancestors' spirits.

When companies and communities sit down to negotiate land compensation, they are often not addressing the same issue

Land is family history and tradition. It is the connection to the past that has value beyond simple memory. Some people believe that they hold their land in trust from those who went before and for those who will come behind. Land represents the inter-generational family and provides continuity from generation to generation.

When companies and communities sit down to negotiate land compensation, they often are not addressing the same issues. For communities, some of these issues go far beyond things that can be bought and sold.

When people keep asking for more money for their land, company managers quite naturally see this as an indication that there is some price that will be satisfactory. They interpret ever-spiraling demands as proof that negotiation is out of control and that people are greedy. What they often do not see is that they need to have a conversation about the *meaning* of land rather than a negotiation over the price of land. Talking about land's meaning could lead to options other than cash payments.

The company sees compensation as a finite process and insufficiently prepares communities for the change in their lives

Companies assume that when they reach a compensation agreement this is the end of their responsibility. They have provided more money to people than most of them have ever seen or given them new resettlement houses that are of much higher quality than people's original dwellings. Managers expect that those who are compensated should demonstrate a little gratitude, and they do not understand when people complain that the corporation did not treat them well.

While communities may initially welcome the improvements in their lives that come with compensation money and houses with better amenities, over time people realize that they have lost not only land but also previous community structure and other non-tangibles they value. Their initial acceptance turns to dissatisfaction as they realize how ill prepared they really were for the changes that compensation brings to their lives. They find it difficult to cope with their new reality.

> ** Yes, it is true, I got a lot of money from the company and they put me in this new house with piped water. But, before, we had free access to bush meat, water, firewood, fruits, and vegetables from our gardens, and many other things that were free. Here in the resettlement village we have to pay for everything, even for toilet paper! Despite the fact that we had little money, we used to know how to manage our lives. We had money but we wasted it and now we are worried about the future. **

> *(Resident of a resettlement village)*

It is becoming standard for companies to compensate for land with land. This approach is meant to ensure that displaced people will still be able to earn a livelihood. The motivation for this approach arises from the evidence of the range of problems that arise when land is compensated with cash. However, land-for-land compensation raises several questions as well. When people value land for continuity and closeness to ancestors, moving poses problems not addressed by the provision of a new plot of land. Even an area that a company considers geographically nearby may seem distant and foreign to local people. Experience shows that it is difficult for newly created resettlement villages to recreate the kind of organic community interactions and spatial relationships that characterize traditional villages that have grown up over many years.

Compensation does not equal livelihood

Some companies also set up alternative livelihood programs as part of their compensation package for people who lose their land. Although the concept of livelihood restoration is gaining ground and increasingly seen as a responsibility of companies, in practice, few companies have made a serious effort to effectively restore the capabilities, assets (both material and social), and activities required for sustainable livelihood. Traditional coping mechanisms related to the former lifestyle by which people dealt with and recovered from stresses such as drought or floods often do not transfer easily into coping mechanisms for dealing with a permanent loss of land or a way of life. Experience to date shows that livelihood programs are often not designed well enough to replace old income streams with new ones, or do so for only a few people.

> Despite the frequent use of words such as sustainable livelihoods, very few companies make serious efforts to effectively restore people's livelihoods

Compensation in the form of cash — even quite generous compensation — also does not ensure a future income stream. Experience shows that large infusions of cash into areas where people have not handled much cash previously often have remarkably negative effects on individuals and communities. Communities tell of the ways they wasted money when they suddenly had cash in amounts they had never before seen. They tell of people altering their lifestyles and spending a lot on consumer items. Once their money was gone, they found themselves impoverished.

In one country . . .

As we drove along the mountainside road, local colleagues pointed out the skeletons of wrecked cars that lay in the valley below. They said that these were the remains of Cadillacs and Mercedes that people had bought with the cash payments they received for their land. Apparently many young men who had no idea how to drive bought a big car and, within days, wrecked it.

A further contributing factor to the unsustainable spending of compensation money is the failure of companies to explain the purpose of compensation money. Companies calculate compensation to cover the time required before a person can gain an equally high income via other means (for example, by cultivating replacement land). But affected landowners often consider the compensation to be extra money that they can use at their discretion without negative consequences.

> ** Imagine how many chickens I have to raise to make up the money my husband squandered on alcohol and canned food when he received his compensation money! **
>
> *(Local woman in a resettlement area)*

Companies and communities operate with differing time horizons

Companies think of land compensation as only one of many early start-up costs involved in launching their projects.

Communities see land compensation as the one, and possibly only and last, legitimate claim they have on company resources.

Companies plan projects over many months and years. Buying land is only one of multiple costs that will be incurred over the lifetime of the project. A manager knows that the company will expend funds in the local community in many ways through hiring, contracting, and community projects.

Small landholders, in contrast, do not know what to expect of the company over the longer term. Instead, they tend to think in terms of maximizing the current benefit. They may not want to sell, but they sense they will have no choice against the big, powerful, and rich company. This may create a sense of desperate urgency — the landholders feel they must get everything they can now, because they see no other legitimate claims on company funds.

Government rules, legal definitions of landownership, and geographical coordinates are inadequate criteria for land compensation

Companies feel that they have little guidance about how to work with communities to find satisfactory compensation plans. Some accept government rules and legal requirements as the appropriate level of compensation. Others simply fall back to government levels if negotiations with community landholders become troublesome.

There are several problems with this approach. Communities often have not been consulted in the establishment of government standards and are therefore unaware of them. Further, many government compensation standards are seriously outdated and do not reflect current value. Government maps may be old and out of date, completely omitting whole communities that have grown up since the maps were drawn. In some countries government regulations stipulate that companies need to compensate only for the loss of crops for one season and do not have to take into consideration future losses for communities that no longer have access to land. Therefore, although payments may be legal, they may not actually compensate appropriately.

> Even when payments are legal, this does not mean they actually compensate appropriately

In many communities, land is not individually owned but is instead an asset shared by tribe, clan, or community. Boundaries are understood through practice and use, not specified on paper. People do not buy land but gain access through traditional systems or usage, assignment by chiefs, or family lineage. As a result, people who have used land allotted to them by traditional means for many generations may not hold a legal deed. They may have never needed to specify exact boundaries. Again, laws governing landownership – which vary widely from country to country – often do not reflect the reality that is experienced and perceived by communities.

Cash payment based on GPS coordinates can undermine shared interests

In one country, hunters and agriculturalists had shared land for centuries. As needs changed, boundaries that were fluid also changed to accommodate family and tribal needs. When the company insisted that it would pay only for designated plots based on global positioning system (GPS) coordinates, battles broke out as people staked out boundaries that had never previously been disputed.

It is far more important to understand who actually uses land for production and how land is traditionally allocated than to simply follow the law

It is not uncommon for legal landowners to live in an urban area and to lease their land to tenants whose rent is a percentage of annual production. When a company compensates the legal owner of the land, tenants who actually lose their livelihoods receive nothing for their losses. One company addressed this by making its compensation payments directly to tenants who then paid a percentage to the owners. When another company announced it would take this same approach, the urban-based legal owners immediately chased their tenants off the land.

When a company is launching a project — and at the same time wanting to establish and maintain good community relations — it is far more important to understand who actually uses land for production and how land is traditionally allocated, than to simply follow the law.

Some of what goes wrong is because of the way a company negotiates

When company managers feel that they need to show they are tough in order to get a good deal, they enter into negotiation focused on achieving the result they see as advantageous to the company. They often negotiate under time pressure specified by the stages of project development.

Although the company may win by being tough, if a community feels muscled into an agreement, the process becomes a source of future difficulties

Traditional communities often value process over results. They have expectations and norms for interactions that include informal conversation on topics unrelated to the focus of negotiations. They emphasize the importance of establishing respectful human relationships to create mutual trust before turning to negotiation.

CEP has seen instances where relatively small differences in what a company offers and what a community asks for lead to protracted and unpleasant negotiations. Although the company may "win" by being tough, if a community feels muscled or tricked into an agreement, the *process* often becomes a source of future difficulties. This situation is compounded when the company enlists the help of a national government official to mediate or a court of law to decide compensation rates. Although this is a reasonable approach in a Western context, it angers communities who are looking for a win-win outcome.

Non-transparency creates inequalities and jealousies

Companies know that they cannot make everyone happy in every community. As they decide on their compensation policies and who deserves payment, they always encounter some people who are dissatisfied.

> Negotiation with each individual landowner often appears faster and easier but can feed into jealousies and divisions

Communities always contain sub-groups who define themselves according to special identities or interests. Individuals belong to multiple sub-groups defined by age, gender, clan, politics, or livelihood, to name a few. At different times, one or another of these multiple identities can become paramount while others seem less important.

Neither companies nor communities recognize that the way a company interacts with communities can reinforce differences and widen dividers between subgroups, making some more important than others, or reinforce and strengthen shared and common identities. (See Chapter 2 on dividers and connectors for a fuller explanation of this point and how it affects company–community relations.)

To acquire land, companies can decide to enter negotiations with each individual landowner or land-owning group, or they can decide to enter negotiations with community representatives who have delegated authority from the landowners but who represent broader community interests as well. Negotiations with individual landowners can seem to be faster and easier, as community representatives often feel that they cannot accept rates that are opposed by some parts of their constituency. However, when companies decide to negotiate with individual landowners in a way that lacks transparency and that uses different standards for different people, it can feed into intergroup jealousies and divisions. These tensions occur when there is a lack of clarity about the criteria used for compensation or when a company pays compensation at their headquarters or in a third location where the details of the transaction are not public. Such tensions not only harm communities; they can also turn around on the company as conflict among community members over allegations of "deal-making" spill over into conflict toward the company.

Dealing with individuals rather than with the community also risks reinforcing a compensation culture as it sends the message that the company is willing to pay whatever it takes to get, and maintain, access to land.

Non-transparency is perceived as trickery

Scenario 1

Thinking he could coerce the reluctant farmers into selling at his price, a site manager made a good deal with a few constructive farmers to demonstrate that this was what he was prepared to pay. Months later, when he finally had to pay more to the remaining difficult farmers who were holding up the project by refusing to sell, the farmers who had entered into early agreements were furious. They felt tricked into accepting a low price without full information. When it came time to begin construction, they blocked the road and would not let the machinery pass. All negotiations were reopened.

Scenario 2

The company carefully paid a fair price for all the land it needed. Those who sold felt comfortable with the settlement. However, their neighbors, whose land lay just outside the boundaries needed by the company, felt aggrieved. They too suffered from a loss of productivity on their land due to pollution by the company, and they suffered inconvenience and disruption from the noise of project operations just next to their homesteads. But the company paid them nothing and did not acknowledge them as among those most impacted. They were furious with the company and with their former neighbors whom they saw as benefiting by selling while they suffered.

Scenario 3

Although the company had made a fair and acceptable settlement with every farmer for his or her land, they made all these agreements privately, meaning to show respect for each farmer. However, since no one knew who had been paid what, rumors began to circulate that two families had been paid much more than all others. Soon, tensions in the community rose to such a point that these families felt threatened by their neighbors.

Options for getting it right

What can a company do to take account of these factors and get the compensation issues right?

Acknowledge cultural attachments to land

Although they may not be able to compensate financially for people's loss in terms of their cultural attachment to land, companies can acknowledge that the loss of land will have a significant impact on people's lives. By having a discussion with people about their connections to their land, the company demonstrates respect for them and their culture. As well, such discussions may generate ideas or options that the company could consider to lessen this sense of loss.

Recognize that interactions with communities about compensation set the tone for many other company–community interactions

Communities stress that the process of decision making about compensation matters as much as the outcome. They want to trust the company and see discussions about land as central to trust. This may require that the company slow down, sit with people in their communities, and listen to how people use and value land beyond its monetary value. Communities who value respect, friendship, and caring learn about a company's attitudes from how the managers behave in negotiating compensation rates.

'If you ask me the right way . . .'

One negotiation between a company and a community over land acquisition extended over a long period of time. Despite a generous company offer, communities did not agree. Several farmers observed, "If you ask me the right way, I will sell you my land for almost nothing, but if I don't like your condescending tone, I won't sell it to you even for a high price." Other people observed that while the company approached the negotiations as a business deal and used formal language, for the community, the loss of land represented an emotional issue. Each side was frustrated by the other's way of approaching the negotiations and by the fact that their efforts to reach a consensus were not acknowledged. As a result, the parties did not reach an agreement.

Balance financial with non-financial compensation

As mentioned earlier, compensating for land with land has now become standard practice. In areas where available land is scarce, companies make agricultural inputs (hybrid seeds and fertilizers) or business inputs (equipment, stock, and technical advice) part of the compensation package. These additions can help farmers increase their yields. Such support is over and above financial compensation for the loss of land and buildings. One company offers this kind of support on the condition that the affected individuals write a business plan. The main objectives of such efforts are that the land allocated to individuals is, at least, sufficient to feed a family and that no person should become destitute when compensation money runs out.

For those that do not want to pursue farming, companies may also help them invest their compensation money in an alternative income-generating activity (such as rental properties in the capital) or contract investment specialists from local banks to provide them with investment advice.

Be consistent in paying compensation rates

In one country, a family received a very large amount of compensation from the company for its land. A few years later, the family told CEP that they would be pleased if the local rebel group would destroy the company because they perceived that they had been cheated by the company as their neighbors got more money than they did two years previously.

Different compensation to different individuals leads to questions regarding fairness. Not paying anyone until everyone in a community has agreed can avoid this problem. Negotiating with landowner representatives can also ensure that everyone feels fairly treated. When negotiating with representatives, it is important to

- Monitor how they are selected to ensure they are chosen fairly and transparently

- Publicize the minutes of negotiation meetings

- Make any agreements transparent

- Arrange for outside experts to conduct skills training for landowner representatives to ensure they are capable of effective negotiation. This training should occur prior to negotiations.

Uniform and agreed-upon rates allow each person to calculate what he or she is owed relative to what others are owed.

Pay promptly and provide help on money management

It is also important that a company pays out all compensation soon after an agreement is reached. The experience is that compensation negotiations take time. But once landowners agree to rates, they want to see their money in the shortest possible time. Prompt payment signals awareness of the disruption that people experience and respect for their needs.

Helping people retain and use their compensation money wisely is also important for a company to signal its longer-term concern with communities' welfare. As noted, experience provides evidence of few alternative livelihood programs that generate sufficient income to replace people's initial compensation money. An increasingly standard practice is to provide financial management training to compensation recipients. Some companies even make attendance at such training mandatory. The key to this approach is that training should occur *prior to*, rather than after, paying compensation because, as one elder succinctly observed, "You cannot tell anything to somebody who has money burning in his pocket."

Some companies have invited community members from other areas who have been paid compensation packages to share their experiences with those who are about to do so, so that people can learn from the mistakes and wise choices of others.

Take an inclusive approach

Some communities note that individual compensation should be kept to a minimum and always be combined with community-wide compensation techniques that benefit larger groups. Examples include educational trust funds, health trust funds, use of compensation monies to start up new enterprises, or technical/vocational training programs.

When companies conduct a vulnerability analysis to determine which groups may proportionally lose out from compensation arrangements (such as renters or landless daily laborers), they can then develop approaches to prevent these groups from becoming destitute. For example, where landowners lease their land to others and the payment for the use of that land has been in kind rather than in cash, it may be appropriate for compensation monies to be divided between landowner and land user.

> Companies conduct a vulnerability analysis to determine the groups that may proportionally lose out

When companies signal to communities outside the direct compensation area that they also will gain from other aspects of company benefits, broader economic linkages to locally initiated enterprises, this may reduce inter-community resentment.

If resettlement is required, help people make the transition

The more disruptive land acquisition is to people's lives, the more important it is for companies to prepare the directly affected people for the change in their lives. Companies use a variety of options.

- **Develop a vulnerability prevention program.** Companies should identify potentially vulnerable people and help increase their coping mechanisms before they lose their land.

- **Monitor how resettled people are faring after they receive their compensation.** One company set up a program to help people settle into their new environment. With the help of an NGO, the company assigned social support workers to visit each family on a regular basis and to monitor and assist their adaptation to the new situation.

- **Help communities visualize the future.** When one company received feedback that communities had difficulties visualizing two-dimensional drawings of their new resettlement homes, it built a few demonstration houses. The same company showed community members a 3-D virtual tour of resettlement homes on the computer.

- **Work with people to re-establish social networks and mutual help strategies.** These networks and strategies help people cope under radically different circumstances. Even when people have money and new houses, if they are cut off from who and what they know, they will be unable to manage. When relocating people, companies should maintain neighborhoods and small communities whenever possible.

- **Invite community members from other areas who have been resettled.** Hold information and question-and-answer sessions to share experiences so people will know what to expect and how their lives will change.

Be transparent

With payments to individuals of any kind, companies should always establish and maintain systems of transparency. When people know what everyone is getting and why, this greatly reduces the possibility of intergroup or community–company tensions around claims of unfairness.

It is important to help people anticipate and prepare for the longer-term aspects of a changed lifestyle that comes from losing their land. People may imagine moving their location without realizing the depth of changes that will follow such a move. Transparent and open discussions of these issues help people prepare and signal that the company takes responsibility for long-term side effects.

Indicators of land compensation effectiveness

- People say they feel fairly compensated and are able to cope with their new lifestyle.

- There is measurable improvement in people's livelihoods (not only financial capital but also physical, human, social, and environmental capital).

- Community leaders say that the company was respectful and understood community concerns during the negotiation process.

- People have used compensation money to invest in income-generating activities.

- There is no intergroup jealousy over the compensation policy.

- People did not become destitute when they lost their land.

8

Contracting policies

Simon, the project manager of a mining site, sighed, "We never seem to be able to get it right. During construction, we worked with an international contractor that was so determined to finish the job on budget and on time that they made promises to communities they could not keep and that we, therefore, inherited. Now, we try to work with local contractors in response to their request to get a slice of the pie, but they keep fighting with each other over who is most local and who is most qualified."

The contracting issue

Most companies contract out many of the activities they previously implemented themselves such as seismic surveys, security, administration, transportation, community projects, and catering. Company managers half-jokingly say that they have become managers of contracting companies rather than producing organizations! The fact that so many company activities are contracted out poses challenges for company–community relations. In some companies, managers estimate that 60–70% of the community challenges they face are caused by contractor behavior.

Communities often have a variety of small-scale enterprises, owned by community leaders who say they can do anything. Local business owners feel that outside contractors, whether national or international, are unfairly awarded contracts when locals could have done the job.

Companies regularly allocate contracts based on evidence of the contractors' competence and the competitiveness of their price, intending to show no preferential treatment for any group. In practice this means that local contractors, especially when they are small and have no experience dealing with large companies, lose out to larger international or urban-based contractors. The latter can order in bulk, are better able to calculate the scope of work, have easier access to capital, and are better equipped to comply with government and safety regulations. They have equipment, staff, management systems, and experience, all of which are important to a project manager who needs assurance that the work will be done on time and to specifications. Very often, tenders are advertised in cities and internationally; local contractors do not even see them before bids are made and accepted.

When outside contractors are hired, their staff rather than company staff can be the first representatives of the company to engage with communities (for example, during seismic surveys). They create the important first impression of a company and of how it will operate and interact with communities.

This combination of community expectations with company and outside contractor incentives means that a company's contracting policies can have a much larger and more lasting impact on the quality of company–community relations than most managers realize.

What goes wrong?

Awarding contracts to outsiders leads to resentment among local businesses and contractors

Companies find it convenient to hire a few large contractors that have established reputations and have worked in similar settings. Smaller local contractors without verifiable track records or that require more administrative oversight are overlooked. Especially when financial stakes are high and the timeline is critical, managers prefer working with larger companies in order to reduce risks of delays and cost overruns. Managers assume that the scope of work will be beyond the reach of local contractors, so they often see no reason to make either bidding or contracting details public.

> Local businesses understand many contracts are out of their reach, but are upset because they never get to see the scope of work at all

Communities feel they should be given preference for contracts since they are most directly affected by a company's presence. When they are overlooked, they blame both outsiders and the company. Locals may try to oust outsiders in order to position themselves for contracting opportunities, and the mutual resentments become the company's problem.

Many local businesspeople say they understand that company contracts are out of their professional reach. But they resent the lack of respect they feel when they are not shown the scope of work in the first place. When local contractors feel entitled to a contract because they are local, they often overestimate their capacity to implement company contracts in accordance with the requisite standards and specifications. They are not aware that company standards exceed local ones, and they lack appreciation of the scale and complexity of the company's plans.

Companies have unclear expectations for contractors' relationships with communities

Companies are hesitant to impose expectations on contractors about their approach to local stakeholders. This is partly because companies are wary of taking responsibility for contractor behavior, over which they have little control.

Communities see contractors, subcontractors, and operating companies as one and the same. They argue that when a company contracts out activities (especially to outsiders) it is only trying to avoid responsibility for the impacts of its implementation. When a company responds to complaints by saying, "It wasn't us, it was the contractor," this sends a message to communities that the company does not want to be held accountable for impacts it considers beyond its control but which occur as side effects of its contracting.

The issue of hiring locally, discussed in Chapter 6, is another area where companies often do not clarify or codify their expectations for contractors. Although many companies say they encourage their contractors to hire locally, only a few make this a contractual obligation. So, when contractors bring in their own staff for work that local communities claim they can do, there is a good chance this will lead to accusations of unfairness.

Some insiders argue that one side effect of not taking full responsibility for contractor behavior is that it provides contractors with an incentive to create community conflict where it did not exist before. Contractors can make *force majeure* claims to their clients if they are unable to work due to community unrest. Such claims can be profitable. In one case encountered by the CEP, a subcontractor was awarded a *force majeure* claim of US$38 million on a contract worth US$130 million.

Contractors work under conditions and incentives that limit consideration of community impacts

The design of large projects often takes place at the offices of engineering companies located in faraway countries. The plans are typically designed one or two years prior to a project's construction. Typically, the engineering processes do not consider what capacity is or could be available in the operational locale.

Local communities (and local contractors) usually learn of missed contracting opportunities only after project designs have been finalized and contracts with international players have been signed. Most efforts to support local contractors are implemented as an afterthought, often when the best conditions for providing local opportunities have passed (for example, after construction is complete). From an external affairs perspective, this is a missed opportunity. Although local contractors typically lack the skills and the managerial capacities to take on large contracts, their roles can be vastly expanded if projects are planned and designed to recognize and utilize local skills and capacities.

> Most efforts to support local contractors are an afterthought when construction has already been finalized

Additionally, companies rely on large international contractors and subcontractors that work on an incentive structure that differs from that of the operational companies. Especially on short-term assignments such as drilling or construction, contracting crews often operate under tight budgets and strict timelines. They may receive bonuses if they complete work "on or under time and on or under budget." Their short-term focus, coupled with short-term incentives, can and often does conflict with companies' interests in establishing long-term, positive relationships with local communities.

Companies use contracts as a tool for community control or as a reward

Some managers hand out contracts to local groups to dampen community threats or to local individuals as a reward for loyalty. Managers who issue such contracts (typically in the form of work orders) tend to award them to the most vocal or obstructive groups in order to maintain a sense of control. They defend their decisions by arguing that it is better to have youth groups working for money than unemployed and causing trouble or that it is good to reward a community leader who is favorable toward the company.

> Awarding security contracts to local youth groups provides an incentive to maintain a level of violence

Groups that do not benefit from these contracts consider such an approach to be bribes or buying peace and, as such, unfair and disrespectful. Over time, other community groups may be encouraged to establish their own entities to make claims on the company's so-called contracts. A company may soon face a proliferation of groups in the community that want (or demand) contracts.

When companies use local contracts to control potential disturbances or problems, this provides an incentive for communities to create a need for such control. Groups may sabotage pipelines in order to receive a contract to clean up oil spills. Groups may threaten company facilities in order to receive a contract to provide protection. In such cases, contracting with locals may ultimately create more uncertainty than it reduces.

In addition, when handing out contracts to local businesses is undertaken as a community-engagement tool — rather than a business proposition — managers have been seen to apply inappropriately lax quality standards. Although it is a good idea to hire local contractors, and it does improve community relations, when a contract is given to satisfy an arbitrarily established goal (such as, 10% of contracts should be for locals) rather than to complete work that is central to company operations, results may go unmonitored and unchecked. Low-quality work done by local contractors can convey company disrespect for communities, especially when the work involves infrastructure that a community needs. For example, if a company pays for a local contractor to put the roof on a school, and the job is badly done, this can feed community conflict and community–company tensions. In some cases, where work was contracted and paid for but not completed, local communities have attacked local contractors and blamed companies for not delivering on their promises and for allowing contractors to engage in corrupt practices.

Administrative requirements are difficult for local contractors

Even when a company favors local contractors to contribute to local economic development, problems can arise that affect company–community relations. For example, in order to comply with government regulations and to reduce risks to the business, a company may require that local contractors are officially registered and have a bank guarantee, liability insurance, and other administrative systems in place.

For most community contractors, such requirements are difficult to meet. Small local businesspeople may have no experience with the legal and governmental departments that provide permits and registrations. When they feel out of their depth and unassisted by the company, some people have claimed that the phrase "preference for local contractors" is nothing more than a hollow public relations slogan offered by a company that really does not care about the community.

An additional contributor to company–community conflict is delayed payment to local contractors. Many local contractors borrow money from relatives or local lenders to pre-finance the costs of the work. If companies delay payments after contract completion (which is not uncommon), high interest rates eat into the contractors' profits, leaving them with little or no cushion to bridge the time until they obtain a new contract. Small local contractors cannot be expected to carry outstanding expenses as large companies can.

" This company says it supports local contractors. But they have delayed my payment now for three months. My suppliers have taken me to court because I cannot pay them as long as the company does not pay me. They don't tell me why I'm still waiting for my money and they keep saying they care about the community. To me, they do not care at all! "

(Local businesswoman)

Options for getting it right

Provide clarity to local contractors about expectations for their work

When the criteria and the decision-making processes for awarding contracts and the results of competitive bids are clear and transparent to local communities, allegations of favoritism, corruption, and deal making will not occur. Managers should:

- **Be transparent about the selection process for awarding contracts** and the capacities and skills required, as well as specifications for project implementation.

- **Organize periodic pre-qualification workshops for local contractors.**

- **Establish an explicit definition of a local contractor in consultation with local communities.** Does the owner need to live locally? Do the staff need to be local? Does the company need to be registered locally?

- **Take local contractors to visit similar projects that have been completed.** There they can observe the scope of work and the quality and safety standards that are required.

Inform local communities about the details of contracts with local contractors

Communities can help to hold local contractors accountable for the quality of their work. In some areas, companies have invited civil society groups to evaluate the effectiveness and quality of community projects on an ongoing basis.

Take responsibility for contractor behavior

An increasing number of companies realize that establishing and maintaining long-term local community support is too important to leave to contractors. As it is standard practice for companies to insist that contractors meet specified safety standards, it is important that they maintain similar rigor in setting standards for behavior towards local communities.

● **Include an annex to contracts stipulating behavioral guidelines for contractor staff.**

● **Specify in the contract the percentage of local staff to be hired for non-skilled positions** (typically between 60–100% of an agreed-to definition of local).

● **Explicitly state expectations with regard to employment and training of locals for more skilled jobs.** One of the criteria of evaluation of bids can be the proposed percentage of local staff contractors guarantee they will employ or the number of apprenticeships they will provide for local youth.

● **Provide assistance to contractors as they develop approaches to communities.** One company successfully organized a one-week team-building exercise between the contractor's construction crew and the operator's crew prior to construction. The effort meant that the construction crew became much more receptive to the advice and suggestions of the operating crew, which had a long-term commitment to the community.

" If it is not in the contract, it does not count (for a contractor)! "

(Director external affairs of a major oil development project)

Integrate local contracting opportunities into the project design and local content strategy

When an external affairs perspective is integrated into construction design and planning, companies may both meet their commercial needs and contribute to local economic development through contracting. Contracting locally provides much-needed employment and plants the seeds for sustained economic growth in the area, contributing to a positive corporate legacy.

A company can take two approaches to providing local contracting opportunities (see Fig. 8.1).

The first focuses on making it easier for existing local contractors to compete with outside contractors. Pre-qualification workshops may provide information on

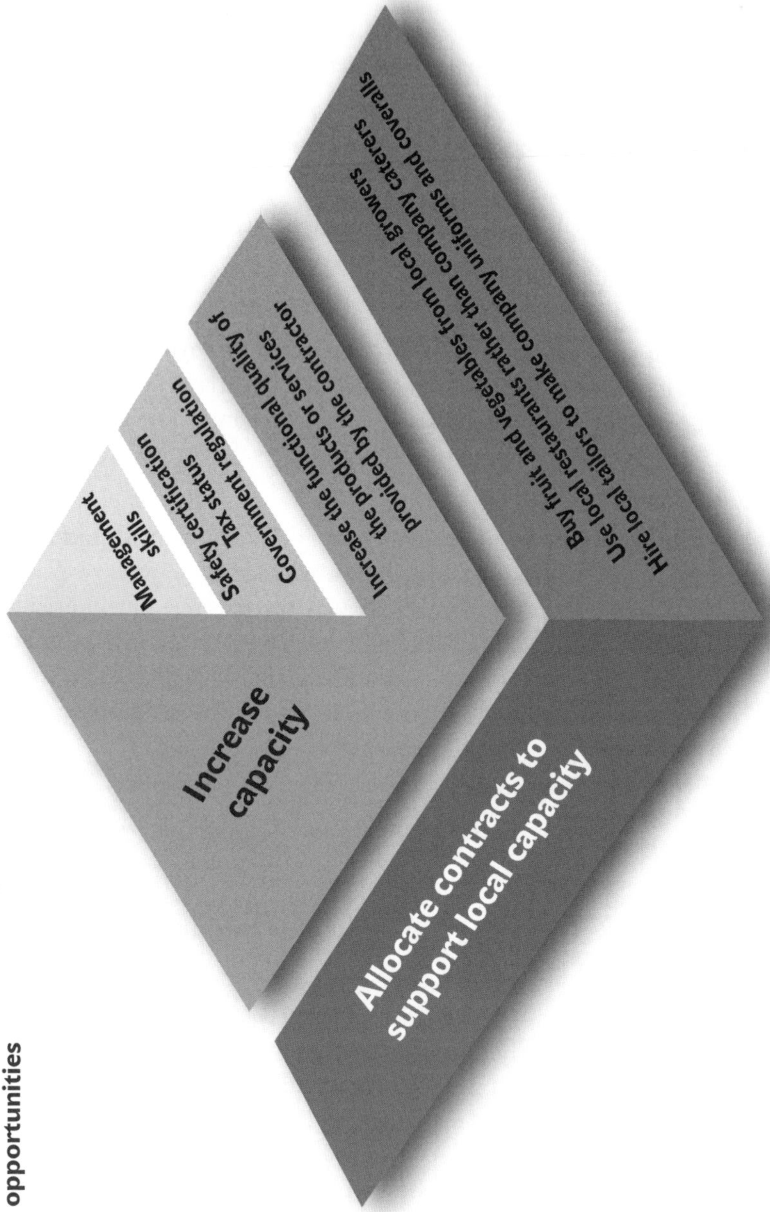

Figure 8.1   **Two approaches to providing local contracting opportunities**

Increase capacity

Management skills

Safety certification

Tax status

Government regulation

Increase the functional quality of the products or services provided by the contractor

Allocate contracts to support local capacity

Buy fruit and vegetables from local growers

Use local restaurants rather than company caterers

Hire local tailors to make company uniforms and coveralls

the specifics of a contract. Some companies give explicit preference to smaller local contractors in every instance where the contract is relatively small and easy to fulfill. Examples include: using local restaurants rather than their own catering service to provide take-out meals for meetings; buying fresh fruits and vegetables for the company dining facilities from local growers; hiring local tailors to make coveralls or uniforms; and hiring local youth to videotape stakeholder-engagement meetings. The list of examples that CEP has seen is long and varied, suggesting that there are many more of these opportunities than companies recognize.

Being aware of high company standards reduces the demand for contracts

One company faced a lot of opposition from local communities who perceived that their contractors did not get any company contracts. In response, the company began weekly training for local contractors to explain how they could meet company standards for safety, administrative requirements, etc. After two months, out of the 25 companies that started the process only one company was left. Many local contractors acknowledged they had underestimated the company requirements and that they were not at the point where they could pursue contracts themselves, especially since the company required any contractor to hire labor locally as much as possible. Thus, local people had a good chance to be hired by outside contractors. As a result of this approach, the community unrest dissolved.

The second approach is one in which companies go a step further by helping local people develop skills that will qualify them to become contractors. Contract aspects of a strategic local-content policy focus on:

1. Building the management skills and capacity of local contractors

2. Guaranteeing that new contractors can meet all safety certifications, tax requirements, and government registration requirements

3. Improving the quality of the products or services potential contractors can provide, often through direct technical assistance

The building blocks of local content

One mining company reckoned it could convince the projects department to use locally made cement blocks for the construction of resettlement houses, company offices, and buildings, if it could demonstrate that local block makers were able to meet company specifications. It assigned an engineer to work with local block makers to adapt their production processes and offered the producers a facility with water and power (constructed by the company but paid for by the producers). The producers were able to meet quality and quantity standards and the project provided incomes for over 60 local youth.

Eight steps to design a strategic local-content plan

1. Start early

Integrating local contracting into project design means starting to work with local stakeholders from a project's pre-feasibility stage. A two-year lead time can help community people prepare to successfully implement contracts even during the construction period. Many local contractors need this much time to be able to meet company standards and specifications.

2. Ensure a community perspective in the project's design process and designate staff to coordinate company requirements with contractor capacities

Some companies add an employee to the design team who both understands the design process and is well versed in community perspectives. This person's job is to ensure that a company's activities contribute maximally to local economic development by identifying all local contracting and employment opportunities and assessing their feasibility.

This person would identify and categorize locally available goods and services and ensure that local contractors get preferences on contracts that are within their reach. This person might actively develop capacities of new contractors. During the design process of a mine, if a company finds that trucking ore is more efficient than building a conveyor belt, it will need dozens of heavy-equipment drivers. Rather than waiting until construction starts and facing a shortage of locally available drivers, this staff person would immediately see an opportunity for training dozens of people to become qualified equipment operators, and, with a local contractor, develop a strategy for the training.

A local-content officer may review the scope of work in all potential contracts and determine if, and how, large contracts can be divided into smaller pieces that local people could perform. In one mine preparation project, contractors were able to bid either on the entire job or only for specific components such as drainage, land clearing, or the like.

Finally, a local-content officer may adjust scheduling of tasks so that local businesses have a flow of work across the year and do not have to lay people off between phases. Large numbers of lay-offs may feed community grievances. Of course, the officer also has the technical expertise to ensure that the critical path of a project is not harmed by dependency on the performance of less experienced contractors.

> ❝ We needed 200 km of pipeline. Instead of using one contractor, we helped organize the various communities along the pipeline route in such a way that we ended up having 100 people each providing 2 km. We then helped them organize themselves so that they approached the pipeline supplier as a group to negotiate a discount. It took some work to organize this process but the project was finished on budget, on time, and without interruption by any of the communities. ❞
>
> *(Project manager)*

3. Allocate costs differently

According to some companies, integrating a local contracting perspective into the project design implies the allocation of the costs of contractor development into the design and construction budget rather than the community projects budget. As some managers note, "We pay twice: first to an outside contractor for work that is needed to run corporate activities and then for development projects to support local contractors that could have done part of the initial work."

Some argue that integrating local economic development activities into the project design can save some costs because local contractors would take over some of the work that otherwise would be done by outside contractors. Further, money earned through employment and contracts would stay in the local area and support economic spin-off activities.

On the other hand, strengthening the capacity of local stakeholders within a defined period of time (for example, two years) requires more human resources compared to approaching local content as a development project, which can be spread over a longer period of time. Also dealing with more, and smaller, contractors requires more supervision and administrative capacity (for example, hiring a local-content officer). And this might add to costs.

Support local content with quality control

An oil and gas company used, as a part of its SOPs, a screening tool to assess the quality and capabilities of contractors and suppliers. Only those that passed the test could become company suppliers or contractors. The company provided weekly coaching sessions to assist companies that failed the test but still wished to become contractors or suppliers. Although intended for quality control purposes, the mechanism provided an effective vehicle for aspiring local contractors to get access to company contracts. At one of the company facilities, a former watchman took the chance to become a contractor and, with the guidance of the company, became the largest local contractor for small-scale electrical work.

4. Remove bureaucratic and administrative obstacles for local contractors

Some companies cover liability insurance for local contractors that would have been too expensive for them otherwise. Other companies help local contractors to register with the government or to comply with the company's safety standards.

5. Provide seed capital to entrepreneurs

Seed capital can be quite small yet crucial in helping a local person become a contractor. It can be as simple as providing a loan to the local sandwich bar to buy a refrigerator to keep produce fresh or to the local taxi driver for an up-to-standards car that can be hired by the company.

6. Reduce the risks for local contractors

Contracting on a costs-plus-margin basis (covering real expenses plus a percentage for labor and profits) can ensure that local businesses do not lose money on contracts because of a poor assessment of the scope of work, late payments, or other obstacles. Another approach is for the company to purchase expensive items such as cement, thereby reducing the financial burden on local contractors to make investments upfront.

7. Build sustainability into a local-content strategy

The construction phase of a project typically lasts only a few years. For a context-specific local-content plan to make lasting contributions to local economic development, it needs to look beyond the construction phase. As one expert said, "Companies can go higher up the food chain." By which he meant they can encourage local contractors to keep improving their capacities so that, over time, they can take on new and larger contracts. This approach has two important benefits. First, as small contractors become bigger and take on larger contracts, it creates space for new contractors to take over the smaller contracts. Second, becoming bigger and better allows local contractors to bid for contracts outside the local area and to be less dependent on the company, improving their chance of survival in the long run.

Sustainability also means that companies have to be competitive. To avoid letting local contractors exploit their privileged position and inflate their profit margins, some companies apply a price cap, paying no more than 10% or 15% over the non-local competition. If local contractors are not able to price themselves within that range, contracts go to an outside contractor.

8. Integrate local content into the corporate management systems

Some companies institutionalize an enterprise development policy that specifies that all contracts will be locally sourced unless it is impossible. Contract officers must certify that they cannot find a local contractor who can meet company standards and project specifications. This justification needs to be specific and can therefore provide valuable information to the group (including the community development department) about the gaps in knowledge or experience among local contractors. A company with an active local-content strategy responds to this information by developing programs to overcome these weaknesses.

Contracting gives companies a good opportunity to provide benefits to local communities. The development of viable local enterprises is a significant advantage of local contracting. When a company recognizes and pursues opportunities for such development it can generate immediate goodwill and contribute to its positive legacy in the lives of local communities.

Indicators of effective contracting policies

- There are fewer complaints about contractor behavior through the grievance procedure.
- Communities credit the company with providing opportunities to local contractors.
- The company receives requests from local contractors for pre-qualification training.
- Local contractors say they understand why they did not obtain a contract.
- There are no *force majeure* claims.

- Local communities acknowledge that the company's local content strategy is in place, with an explicit target about the contracting volume the company wants to source locally within a number of years.

- Communities acknowledge the increasing volume of contracts being locally sourced.

- Local contractors say they are increasingly able to get subcontracts from the company's larger contractors.

- Local contractors say they are increasingly able to get contracts outside the company.

9

Community consultation and negotiation

Gloria had a problem. Her company believed that contact with local communities should be minimal. They had had bad experiences. Each time they organized a meeting with community representatives, the community demanded more and more. After many months, Gloria had finally been able to convince her colleagues that she should organize a public meeting as a gesture of goodwill. But, after barely ten minutes, some youths started accusing the company of making secret deals with the wrong community representatives. When the young people started to shout, Gloria's security colleagues swiftly evacuated her. They vowed there would not be another public meeting until Gloria could make sure that these youths were going to behave in an orderly way.

The community consultation issue

Most managers find community consultation a muddy and challenging aspect of their work. There are few legal requirements — or conditions imposed by project finance institutions — about community consultation other than that it *must* take place. Few guidelines exist laying out *how* to interact with communities. Companies recognize that communities are important stakeholders in that they both are affected by and able to influence corporate activities.

Broadly speaking, company–community consultation takes three different forms:

1. **Informal discussions in community venues,** at sports events or weddings, in the local bar or through company-organized weekly visits. Such informal interactions serve the important purpose of maintaining an ongoing friendly relationship.

2. **Periodic corporate-sponsored open-ended discussions,** town-hall meetings or public information sessions with stakeholders. Such events provide a place for exchange of ideas and soliciting perspectives and opinions that can inform the company's actions. They are not intended to arrive at formal agreements.

3. **Negotiations** where a series of meetings is deliberately convened to reach an agreement on a particular issue.

These different forms are complementary; one does not substitute for the others. Through some forms of engagement a company provides information to stakeholders, whereas others require that the company adopt a listening role. Different community members need different engagement strategies, in terms of both the frequency and the format of meetings. For those most directly affected by a company's operations, face-to-face meetings can be the most appropriate. For people less directly affected – such as the larger community, politicians, or journalists – open houses, public forums, and written documentation can be better.

> Often, more constructive discussions take place in teashops than in conference halls

When a formal engagement encounters obstacles, continuing or intensifying the informal processes can be especially valuable. Often, more constructive discussions take place in teashops than in conference halls.

Generally, a company's interaction with local stakeholders starts well. Communities are eager to meet and know the company, and they welcome opportunities to see them in action.

What goes wrong?

Companies wait too long to start a consultation process

Many managers hold off engagement with communities until they have to respond to specific problems or issues that affect the company's ability to operate. In the busy start-up days, community consultation is not their top priority. They fear that consultation will be too time-consuming when other matters are more pressing against the tight deadlines they face. Some undertake community consultation only to meet an external requirement for a social impact or environmental analysis. Others assume that consultations will result in demands on company assets and that, if they are not available, people will not be so demanding. Other managers feel that they need to have all the answers for expected questions before they meet community members. They postpone consultations and miss an opportunity for generating options and creative ideas for unresolved issues.

Communities, on the other hand, point out that the failure to consult costs companies more in project delays than would have been the case had the company had reached out to them early. Communities that were initially positive about a corporate arrival interpret the reluctance of company managers to interact as untrusting and disrespectful.

> Community consultation as crisis management is destined to fail

But companies cannot ignore communities forever. Starting an engagement process too late means that a company will be forced by local communities to engage when problems start to emerge. At that point, a manager will no longer have the initial goodwill the company's arrival fostered. When problems are acute, a manager will also find it difficult to gain access to local or international partners who could have assisted consultation efforts, such as local leaders or humanitarian NGOs. This is because NGOs that work with a company known to disrespect local people open themselves to reputational risks by doing so. As a result of delaying consultation, a manager may be forced to begin tense negotiations with a disappointed and hostile community, relying on staff who have little experience with or credibility for working with communities. Community consultation as crisis management is destined to fail.

A company focuses on outcomes more than on processes

When company staff regard engagement solely as a means of achieving a specific result, they engage with local communities in the same way they negotiate a business deal with another company. Obtaining signatures on agreements or finalizing terms of compensation then become the primary objectives.

Managers of companies that take such a negotiation-focused approach assume that engagement is necessary but that it need not address core operational issues. In order to work toward and maintain maximum control over a desired outcome, they design a quick negotiation process with limited stakeholder representation. Participation is restricted either to those who are potentially the most obstructive or to the most influential people capable of swaying community support. Agendas are fixed to control the outcome.

As a result of the way meetings are set up, company staff often find themselves sitting on the opposite side of the table from community people, both literally and figuratively. The company tries to give in to community demands as little as possible, and communities negotiate hard to obtain maximum benefits. The negotiation focus is typically on short-term benefits such as jobs, contracts, infrastructure projects, or various forms of financial compensation.

Managers are surprised when such negotiations become recurring events with progressively increasing community demands. In response, the company reduces or minimizes community engagement, fearing that more engagement will always lead to ever-higher demands and expectations.

> Companies consider consultation part of a business transaction; communities value the process of establishing a long-term relationship

Over and over, communities describe the value of process over outcome. They note the importance of both informal and formal interaction with companies. Negotiations around specific issues are viewed as only one part, and not the most important part, of the company–community relationship. They want to establish a long-term relationship with the company rather than constantly haggle over projects and benefits. How the company engages with people is equally, if not more, important to local people than the outcome of the engagement. By focusing on winning, companies often overlook the interaction process and leave unaddressed the problems that created the need for negotiations. Until these problems are addressed, communities will raise them again and again. Some communities have explained that the escalation of tensions and of their negotiation demands are a *result* of limited interaction and communication with corporations. They seek to have all their needs addressed whenever the company doors are open precisely because they are so often closed.

When companies relate to stakeholders only when things go bad, it becomes almost impossible for both parties to soften their respective hard-line positions. It is difficult for them to get to know each other on a personal level or to focus on common objectives. Both parties miss opportunities for constructive engagement. Communities' beliefs about the company — that the company does not care about local stakeholders, wants to minimize benefits to local communities, and is only interested in maximizing profits — are reinforced.

Perhaps not surprisingly, the CEP visits found that where the quality of day-to-day relationships between companies and communities was poor, community demands were much higher than in situations where company–community relations were positive.

Companies deal with the wrong community representatives

One of the main challenges for company managers is identifying genuine, appropriate representatives of any community. In some cases, traditional authorities exist but are weak. Many individuals or groups clamor for the company's attention and present themselves as community representatives. When such individuals come to the corporate office, speak a Western language, are formally educated and knowledgeable about local laws and customs, it is tempting for managers to assume they are legitimate community representatives, especially when there is no other apparent authority and no unified community leadership.

> When community representatives speak a Western language, are formally educated, and articulate, it is tempting for managers to assume they are legitimate

Communities point out that individuals who most readily present themselves, and who look and sound like company staff, are often elites who do not represent them. These people often position themselves between the company and the community for their own gain, and this works to the detriment of both the company and the community.

Some managers feel they have no choice but to deal with people who display negative authority, such as armed groups who threaten violence, kidnap staff, or destroy company property. However, by dealing with such negative leaders, companies legitimize them and feed into conflict by rewarding violence over peacefulness and rationality.

In fragmented communities, it is difficult for company managers to determine how many representatives they should deal with. In communities where some groups have been historically favored and others marginalized, the company's choice of leaders can reinforce marginalization and intergroup divisions.

Dealing solely with elected officials is no guarantee that the company is responding to broad community interests. For example, politicians may have won elections by buying support or because of low voter turnout or a lack of widespread support for alternative candidates.

A company's arrival may spark leadership conflicts, fragmentation of communities, and accusations that the company, by its choice of whom to consult, is disrespectful and manipulative. Company failure to ensure that marginalized groups are represented can provide a platform for politicians, advocacy groups, or, in some cases, guerrilla groups or criminals to stir up anti-company sentiment.

The company is represented by the wrong people

Companies sometimes use government intermediaries to deal with local communities. Where communities perceive the power imbalance between themselves and the government to be overwhelming, they resent this. To them, it shows that the company does not care about them.

Often companies rely on staff who have lived in an area for a long time and who speak local languages to conduct all community interactions. It is logical to choose such people as company–community liaisons. However, there may also be a downside to complete reliance on a few seasoned staff. In some places, CEP has found that, while experience and understanding of the local context are assets, they can also produce fixed positions and tired expectations. Sometimes, a person who feels that she or he has seen and heard it all before has trouble listening to new issues with fresh ears. This can limit creativity and community respect.

Staff representing the company in formal negotiations should be different from those engaged in day-to-day consultations

Confusion or the merging of roles may also pose problems for company–community consultation. CEP has seen instances in which the same company personnel are involved in both informal day-to-day consultations as well as in formal negotiations with communities. In some instances during a negotiation process, tensions escalated and offensive remarks were made on both sides. These dynamics then affected company–community relations outside the negotiation process. When a company representative was perceived as arrogant and bullying during negotiations, it affected broader community responses to that person – and to the company – in informal discussions. Similarly, the unpleasant negotiation formed the basis of company representatives' opinions about their community counterparts whom they saw as domineering and unreasonable. This limited their ability to see opportunities for constructive engagement with the larger community.

Community consultation and interaction take place at the wrong venue

Companies often prefer to hold meetings with community stakeholders at the company offices. This saves time for company staff who do not have to travel, and it provides a more controlled environment for the consultation or negotiation. Although the company may provide seating allowances to compensate community representatives for their travel time, holding all meetings at the company site conveys several negative messages. Communities may perceive that companies do not respect local hospitality. It can convey an imbalance of power.

Meeting solely at the company premises sends the signal that the company is too arrogant to visit those it claims to care about

When company–community engagement takes place exclusively at the company site, the wider community cannot observe what happens. This leads to rumors. Communities worry that company officials are making payoffs to community representatives to achieve favorable outcomes. Whether this is true or not, such perceptions undermine the credibility and legitimacy of community representatives and the company. And, when people do not feel involved in the discussions, they do not take ownership of decisions that are made on their behalf.

In addition, meeting solely at the company premises sends the implicit message that power sits with the company, and stakeholders have to come as supplicants to the company. This is often taken as proof that the company is too arrogant to visit the communities it claims to care about.

Options for getting it right

A company's business goes more smoothly when company staff and community representatives work as partners to solve common problems and achieve common goals. CEP finds many managers want to establish such relationships but simply do not know how to do so.

Three elements of engagement

As a basis for getting it right, it is important to understand the elements of engagement. Companies can learn about this from an analytical tool regularly used by people in the conflict resolution field.[3] Positive engagement requires three elements: relationship, procedure, and content (Fig. 9.1). All three need to be addressed — and in the right order!

Company–community engagement will not gain the local support a company needs if communities feel they are not genuinely listened to and acknowledged. The basis for positive engagement is a strong and respectful relationship.

Once parties have established a relationship, there needs to be clarity and agreement on the procedures of engagement. This includes details such as who represents the community, who represents the company, and when and where various forms of engagement take place.

When companies and communities take the time to develop a positive relationship and together work out a set of procedures for discussing different types of issues, they will find their interactions — even on difficult problems — respectful and productive.

> Addressing all three elements of stakeholder consultation allows for a shift from sitting on opposite sides of the table to sitting side by side

---

3   Chris Moore, *The Mediation Process: Practical Strategies for Resolving Conflict* (San Francisco: Jossey-Bass, 2nd edn 1996). This framework was found to be sufficiently helpful that CEP has adapted it here.

Figure 9.1 **The three elements of engagement**

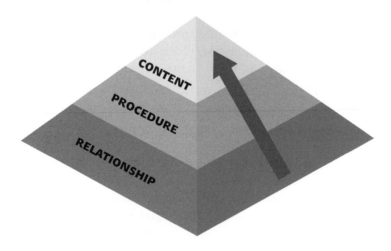

Addressing all three elements of community consultation — relationship, procedure, and content — allows company and community to avoid (or shift from) a reactive negative spiral of opposition and to build (or move) toward working on common goals.

Invest in building trust

Managers need to rid themselves of the assumption that communities are mainly interested in tangible benefits and tangible outcomes. Respect and trust are high priorities for communities and the processes of establishing respect and trust are important components of community consultation. Investing in building trust involves a change of approach and a commitment of time. The best advisors on how to build trust are in the community. As previous chapters have outlined, communities are clear and precise about how the positive elements of relationships are built (see Table 9.1).

Start consultation early, ensure it is ongoing, and show patience in the early stages

Experience shows that it takes time to develop relationships that demonstrate respect and trust. Informal interaction and listening to community ideas are critical elements of relationship building. When a manager spends some time in community consultation that is not intended to produce a binding negotiated agreement, it helps build a relationship, which is ultimately likely to reduce the time and direct costs of subsequent negotiations.

Table 9.1 **Actions that can build trust or break it** (continued over)

Trust builders	Trust breakers
Benefits distribution • Company is reliable and predictable; it follows through on commitments/promises • Community meets company staff in informal and personal settings even when there is no decision to be taken about benefits distribution • Community people have direct access to company decision makers who determine benefits distribution • Company is seen as trying to generate maximum benefits for local people • Community is well informed about future prospects or plans • Company is clear about criteria for distribution of benefits both before and after distribution	• Company does not follow through on commitments/promises • Company engages with the community only when it wants something or when the community behaves in an obstructive manner • Company does not respond to letters and/or community requests • Company deals with "representatives" who lack community support • Company makes deals in secret • Company plays groups with different interests off against each other
Behavior • Company staff respect local culture, social and religious norms, and values • Traditional leaders such as elders or local dignitaries are treated with traditional respect • Company shows respect for culturally significant sites • Company uses language that people understand • Expatriates speak at least some words of the local language • Staff do not seem hurried or impatient with local people (take time to listen in meetings, drive slowly through towns and greet people, etc.) • Company regularly acknowledges that it needs the community's involvement for a project to be successful	• Company staff violate cultural and religious norms and values • Company managers use legalistic or scientific language that communities do not understand • Company staff behaviors are flashy or wasteful • Company is seen to maintain close relations with oppressive or corrupt authorities • Company has a high security profile, visiting communities only when accompanied by security forces or having a strongly armed presence at the company gate

Table 9.1 (from previous page)

	Trust builders	Trust breakers
Side effects	• Company acknowledges likely side effects of its location and operations and works with communities to prepare for and manage these • Company immediately takes responsibility for any environmental impacts and works with communities to mitigate these • Company is seen to help out with small problems for people beyond its immediate business interests (e.g., staff come out to work with a community on a community work day) • Company maintains an accessible and responsive mechanism by which the community can hold the company accountable for side effects • Communities are regularly consulted and have a say in solving problems as they arise	• Company addresses symptoms of problems rather than basic causes (e.g., it compensates for oil spills but does not clean up thoroughly) • Company provides no information about likely negative impacts of its presence or regarding day-to-day issues, future plans, or how decisions are made • Company is paternalistic in solving problems rather than working with communities to come up with best solution

Experience shows that it also takes a considerable amount of time to explain a project's plans and to help people understand how those plans will affect their local context. This is the case especially in communities that have not experienced anything of comparable magnitude to new company operations. By recognizing community rights and people's concerns about the changes that a large-scale project will bring to their lives, and allowing people time to understand these changes before they become a reality, companies demonstrate that the community is a partner in their planning. Some managers, as a rule of thumb, begin a community-engagement process two years before the first bulldozers roll into the community.

Stakeholder engagement is a continuous process and should not be used only in case of a crisis

When company liaison officers visit communities regularly, at specified times, they can disseminate information informally and listen for local issues or rumors as they arise. Frequent and predictable visits also enable liaison officers to gain the confidence of and establish friendships with local people. Any grievances may also be addressed at an early phase before they escalate into conflicts or tensions.

When companies maintain accessible and open relationships with communities through regular consultations, the latter do not feel they need to express all their demands or press for maximum benefits at any one meeting. They know they will have other opportunities to discuss issues and be heard. Attention to relationship building and to the processes of engaging with communities pays off by preventing many problems and laying the groundwork of trust for solving problems that do arise.

Locate community consultations wisely

Companies and communities can engage in any of three locations: in the community, at the company premises, or at a neutral third location. Each location has some advantages and some disadvantages. When deciding between community and company premises, companies should consider some of the factors listed in Table 9.2 when deciding where to hold different kinds of meetings or consultations.

Different venues suit different forms of engagement. When individual community members want to discuss individual grievances, company premises may provide the most privacy. On the other hand, if a group of people who find it difficult to travel from the village have a concern, then a meeting in a location that is convenient for them makes more sense. Issues that concern the larger community might be informally discussed around the football field or in a local tea shop or, more formally, in the community center or church. A company-sponsored information meeting, intended to inform community leaders of upcoming plans, may best be held at a nearby hotel. In all cases, the company should consider the convenience of the community and ensure that the location chosen best communicates the company's commitment to transparency and inclusion in discussions.

One clear observation coming out of CEP is that companies that ensure they have a regular and ongoing presence in the community tend to have more productive communication with communities than those who mainly engage at the corporate premises.

If conditions make open consultation difficult, companies can nonetheless find strategies for maintaining some communication with communities. Where a repressive government might be wary of public gatherings and open discussions, companies have found ways to engage. Some strategies include the following:

- **Negotiating with the government to allow the creation of elected village communication committees.** These committees would be established solely to discuss company–community affairs such as social programs on the condition that they do not become involved in politics.

- **Introducing suggestion boxes.** These can be effective in some contexts. However, in areas where people may fear that suggestions will be read by spies, a company would have to establish a system that reassures villagers about who is emptying the box and who reads the messages.

Table 9.2 **Where to hold meetings**

	In the community	At the company premises
Advantages	• Keeps consultation transparent. Community members can witness the consultation process, listen to discussions, and gain information about how benefits will be allocated • Increases accountability of local leaders. Community members identify their own representatives and monitor whether they speak on their own behalf or not • Decreases the risk that consultation is dominated by only a few individuals • Signals the value of broad community input and involvement • Contributes to community ownership of the consultation process and its outcomes	• Provides a company-controlled environment • Enables the company to explain its plans in more detail • Enables the use of presentation technology and visual aids (e.g., PowerPoint, video) to get a message across • Minimizes potential for disturbance, threats, and pressure to make concessions • Saves travel time for company managers
Risks	• Certain individuals' points of view can disrupt or dominate a meeting and, sometimes, mean that the company is not able to present its message • Arguments among community members may unnecessarily escalate tensions in relation to company matters • Increases the risk that the company can be bullied by public pressure • Can pose security risks or make security personnel nervous	• Contributes to the public perception that staff is not willing or is too arrogant to meet in the community • Can lead to rumors and miscommunication among community people who are not present • Can lead to accusations that community representatives are corrupt • Makes it difficult for the company to verify the degree of community support for the position of representatives who come to meetings

- **Assigning staff to conduct regular home visits.** Staff could collect statistics or disseminate public health information on a one-on-one basis and at the same time learn about and gain a good sense of the social and political issues in the community. These staff should be women where access to local women is important.

Engage and legitimize appropriate community representatives

Although stakeholder representation is often complex, the following approaches can help managers better identify and work with appropriate community representatives.

Learn about and follow local protocol

Every society has its own protocol for receiving newcomers. In some places, new and important visitors introduce themselves to the mayor. In other contexts, traditional authorities are the first group who should be visited. Local communities note that it is important for a company to follow the local system in order to demonstrate respect for local traditions, even if in some places these dignitaries have little power in the community or are not respected. If traditional authorities have little power or respect, it is important that the company deal both with them and with others.

Following protocol

In one community where a major company had been working for decades, the CEP team joined a local NGO in a visit with local authorities that were severely under-resourced. The few staff had not been paid for months. This visit was the first time in nine (!) years that any outsider had visited the office. Community members explained that, although they considered the officials powerless and ineffective, the fact that this delegation followed protocol sent an important signal of respect to the larger community.

Work through the traditional decision-making system

Community decision-making mechanisms differ significantly around the world. Some company managers assume that decision-making power rests in a single community representative when, in fact, often such power resides in a group such as a family, clan, or entire tribe. To ensure that decisions are legitimate in the eyes of the broader community, companies should understand local systems.

Listen to how people describe the representatives they trust

This is best done by simply asking community members who represents their interests or whose promises or ideas they believe. Companies need to find out how people who claim to be community leaders have derived, and how they maintain, their positions. Again, this is easily done by asking local people. It is important to be particularly alert to the possibility that representatives are self-appointed and gain support only through their ability to extract benefits from the company through confrontation.

Engage with both formal and informal leaders and balance these relationships

Each community has both formal and informal authorities who are respected by the population. As it is important to follow protocols with formal leaders, it is also useful to engage informal leaders in informal ways, such as inviting them to serve on an advisory board or inviting them to company dinners and celebrations.

Identify people who want to make a positive difference

Listening for and working with people who have inclusive ideas about how to make life better for entire communities (rather than only for sub-groups within the community) reinforces positive connectors and diminishes the likelihood of constant competition for company benefits among groups.

Be inclusive and broad in defining representativeness

Inclusiveness reinforces the idea that the company cares about and wants to be responsive to the broad community rather than favoring and benefiting the few.

Work with those who want to make a positive difference

A company worked close to a community where there was a leadership vacuum. When considering a program to support renovation of a local school, the company invited anyone who was interested to planning meetings. Some community members who were embarrassed by the lack of leadership shown by their official representatives took the initiative to organize themselves around the school renovation. Without any help from the official leaders, this group managed to carry out the school project. This gave them great satisfaction as they saw they had worked to benefit the entire community.

Establish systems to ensure that representatives remain accountable to the broad community

Some companies agree with communities on term limits for elected committee members. This not only broadens representation over time, it also maintains a high level of accountability for leaders.

Ensure consultation outcomes reach everyone who needs to know

One lesson managers have learned the hard way is that community representatives do not necessarily communicate the outcomes from company–community consultations. Companies should develop systems of transparency to ensure information reaches the broadest possible community. To ensure broad information flows:

Agree with community representatives on a system for disseminating outcomes

Some companies agree with community representatives that the latter will always organize a public debriefing after each important company–community meeting. Company staff attend this debriefing both to ensure that the community is well informed and to clarify any points of uncertainty or confusion.

Keep records of consultations and make these public

Some companies publish minutes of all meetings they have with community representatives and make these records easily available on public bulletin boards or in local newspapers. Other companies video all community consultations and replay these in villages and venues where anyone who wishes can observe what happened. Such public disclosure not only ensures broad communication of results, it also reinforces accountability of both the company and of community representatives to the broader community population.

Recognize the importance of local staff as information disseminators

Communities around company operations base their perceptions of and attitudes toward the company on the stories they hear from their neighbors who work for the company. For companies, this means that the community starts *inside* the company premises. By ensuring that they consistently inform local staff on all relevant issues, they can create opportunities for improving ongoing community consultation. One creative company organized role-playing sessions for its staff. They practiced how to explain the company's grievance procedure to their neighbors. A well-informed workforce serves as an effective dissemination source to local communities. It also provides the company with an up-to-date sense of community perspectives.

Prepare for community meetings and establish ground rules that fit the purpose of the meeting

Companies that use public meetings as a main venue for interaction with communities stress the importance of preparation to ensure a good outcome.

Explain to communities early that meetings will be ongoing so that people do not feel that they have only one chance to be heard

Ensure that everyone in the community is informed about meeting times and content

People should have time to arrange to be there and know about the content of the proposed agenda so they can prepare for the topics of discussion. Use a variety of means to publicize meetings (e.g., bulletin boards, fishing associations, markets, mosques, and churches) to be sure to reach everyone.

Arrange meetings at times and locations where the people who need to be there can come

This means that public meetings must not be held during work days or during times when women are cooking or putting children to bed. For smaller meetings with representatives, find out whether people need a seating allowance or lost-day compensation to participate.

Ask community leaders to suggest topics that they would like to discuss

This will help the company prepare for these topics.

Clarify the company and community expectations for this specific meeting

For example, some meetings have an information purpose only, while others are intended to make decisions or reach agreements. Making expectations explicit and clear allows both company and community to hold each other accountable and keep expectations realistic.

Take a step-by-step approach

Although broad consultation is always the rule, sometimes it makes sense to prepare for large consultations by meeting with smaller groups first.

> " I fear that if we organize a public meeting on this issue too quickly, certain community members will dominate the meeting and it will end up in a mess. Instead, we will take a step-by-step approach and first organize meetings at the company premises for specific groups such as farmers, religious leaders, or chiefs, thus enabling a discussion in a more controlled environment. Once these constituencies are better informed about the facts, we can have a discussion with the whole community. "
>
> *(External affairs director of a mining company)*

Carefully select company representatives

It is clearly the responsibility of all company staff to engage amicably with local communities on an informal basis. Deciding who should interact on behalf of a company in more formal engagements, such as public consultations and negotiations, involves several additional considerations.

Personalities count!

A community's general perception about a company is largely influenced by the behaviors and approaches of the key corporate spokespeople who are present in formal community meetings. It is important for corporate headquarters to recognize that personality matters as much as technical experience in such interactions. (This point is often missed by company human resource departments. See Chapter 13 on internal management issues that affect company–community relations.)

Ensure that staff roles are delineated when requirements for roles conflict

One company observed that tensions with key representatives that arose during negotiations started to negatively affect informal and day-to-day engagement with the wider community. Managers decided to use different staff for the two separate channels. Relationships improved considerably as the community started to see the negotiations as a separate process that no longer tainted its positive day-to-day relationship with the company.

Select staff who are comfortable with conflict and have strong listening skills

When negotiations are predicted to be difficult, the company should ensure that its representatives are not flustered by conflict or tensions but are able, even in heated circumstances, to listen (and be seen to be listening) carefully and respectfully to disagreeing positions. Remaining calm and respectful under attack is a primary skill for company personnel who are involved in community consultation on issues where feelings run high. It is important for such staff to listen as much as they speak and to avoid making assumptions about what the other side means without first verifying that they fully understand.

> One important rule is to listen as much as you speak and to avoid making assumptions without verification

Disaggregate large issues into smaller components

Companies tend to negotiate to achieve broad goals, such as agreement on compensation rates or conditions of a mine closure. When managers are able to disaggregate such broad goals into component parts, they set up interim opportunities for meeting expectations, gaining credibility, and building trust. Short-term, tangible progress can be visible and reassuring. A staged approach also allows groups of stakeholders to become accustomed to and comfortable with the negotiation process.

Learning to negotiate

One community leader noted that the biggest contribution the company made to his life was teaching him how to negotiate. He explained that this educational process has increased self-confidence among communities and positioned them to deal more effectively with the government and with other companies. He concluded, "Business development is not about money or about setting up a transportation company tomorrow; it is about explaining how things work, step by step."

One company found that negotiations floundered because community members did not understand the basic principles of negotiations. They were constantly worried that the company was trying to cheat them. The company engaged a local university, an independent and credible body, to provide a two-day training course attended by both the company negotiators and the community representatives. The negotiation process proceeded much more smoothly after this training.

Recognize non-monetary aspects of negotiations

It is important for companies to be sensitive to underlying interests that drive the community points of view. Groups might call for financial or other tangible benefits such as jobs, contracts, or community projects because these are the terms of discussion offered by a company. However, more subtle and personal concerns may be of equal or greater importance.

Distinguish positions from underlying interests

Negotiations were under way over crop compensation rates. Scarcity of land meant the company was not able to offer alternative land to farmers who lost their plots. The company offered compensation well above rates offered by companies in other parts of the country, but people continued to demand more and more money. Informal discussions finally revealed that money was not the issue. In the farmers' culture, land determined identity, community status, and heritage. As one farmer asked, "What is a farmer without land?" Once the company recognized that identity and heritage were threatened by the sale of land, they acknowledged this to the farmers. Then they were able to have a conversation about options addressing the farmers' interests. Together, the farmers and the company developed a package that satisfied both the material and non-material concerns of the farmers.

Develop the technical expertise of the community on the issues at stake

One company negotiator spent a considerable amount of time providing local representatives with technical and financial information about the basics of mining (for example, explaining what a daily production of 4000 tons meant), payback structures, returns on investment, and the like. He believed that, if the community representatives felt fully informed, they would have greater confidence in their negotiating ability and greater trust that they would not be tricked by the company. One community negotiator later noted, "With the information provided, I was able to go back to my community and confidently explain what we could reasonably expect and what was simply unrealistic to demand."

Summary

If managers are prepared to adapt their approach along the lines shown above, Figure 9.2 summarizes how managers can get it right or get it wrong in community consultation.

Indicators of effective community consultation

- People say they feel listened to and that the company takes their concerns seriously.

- People say the consultation process is respectful, participatory, and inclusive.

- Minority groups in the community say they feel their interests are represented.

- Both company and community say the other is their partner, not an opponent.

- There are no sabotage, work interruptions, etc., due to community unrest.

Figure 9.2 **Community consultation requires a shift in managers' approaches**

Community consultation requires a shift in managers' approaches	
GETTING IT WRONG	**GETTING IT RIGHT**
Meeting communities when there is an immediate crisis or demand (reactive)	Meeting on an ongoing basis to prevent a crisis situation (proactive)
Community and company have different goals and objectives, and sit "on opposite sides of the table"	The company and the community are sitting "side by side" to focus on identifying and achieving shared goals and objectives
A focus on short-term and tangible demands such as jobs, contracts, infrastructure projects, and hand-outs	A focus on addressing long-term goals, achieved by strengthening the capacity of the community to meet its own aspirations
The community does not trust the company's long-term commitment and wants maximum immediate benefits	Both the company and community aim to generate optimal benefits
Engagement around negotiations only	Engagement through informal meetings and consultation
The company provides limited information based on the assumption it can be used against the company	The company shares information based on the assumption that partners have to work together
Focus on outcome	Focus on the process with the expectation it will lead to a good outcome
Budget-driven: "What can we do given the limited and predetermined budget?"	Needs-driven: "What resources are needed to materialize our objectives?"

Special note on establishing grievance procedures

Grievances are an inevitable part of any project. Companies must learn to expect and plan for disagreements and problems rather than treating them as abnormal and unfounded. The establishment of a transparent and predictable grievance procedure is an important component of an effective community consultation process. An effective grievance procedure provides an indispensable tool for communities and companies to address difficulties in a non-confrontational manner. As noted, when stakeholders feel they have no mechanism for addressing problems in a peaceful manner, they turn to confrontation. Figure 9.3 shows how a grievance procedure can be broken down into different components.

> When stakeholders feel they have no mechanism to address their grievances in a peaceful manner, they turn to confrontation

The key principle to designing a grievance procedure is *respect* for those submitting grievances. The process of handling a grievance is equally, if not more, important to the complainant than the outcome. There are six characteristics of a respectful grievance procedure:

1. The process must be clear and transparent

The overall progression of a grievance procedure must be transparent, understandable, and open. There should be clarity about the nature of the complaints that can be lodged, where and how people can file a grievance, when the company will provide feedback, and in what manner. A description of the procedure needs to be disseminated widely and written in plain language and, if necessary, in multiple languages to ensure broad understanding. For illiterate groups, information about the procedure should be made available through video presentations or radio or other oral communication techniques. Decisions about grievance outcomes should be publicly posted and available for review. The reasons for the outcome of the investigation should be clearly presented in the language(s) commonly used by the community.

The company should provide feedback to the person who submitted the grievance at each stage of the procedure. At the initial stage, there should be a mechanism to assure complainants that their grievances have been received by the company.

Figure 9.3 **Anatomy of a grievance procedure**

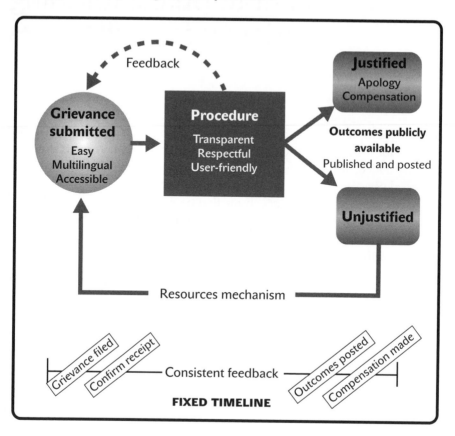

2. The procedure must be accessible

The place where people can submit a grievance needs to be public and available to anyone in the community. In areas where people are widely dispersed, there should be more than one location for submitting grievances. Some companies put their grievance registers outside the company premises to allow community members to file them without passing through security checkpoints. If grievances can be submitted verbally, the company must assure the community that complaints will be communicated to the right person(s). Forms and processes need to be simple and clear.

3. Submitting a grievance must be safe and be seen to be safe

No one should face any danger or penalty for submitting a grievance. The company must make it clear that it is willing and eager to hear the community's grievances. The company must respect requests for anonymity.

4. The process should be predictable and include a timeline

People need to know what to expect when they file a grievance. They should know the status of the grievance at any given time. There should be a fixed and understood timeline for the entire process. People should know when and how the company will respond to them to and how they can inquire about the status of a grievance. If, for any reason, the company is unable to respond to a grievance within their specified time limit, they must provide an explanation to the person who submitted the grievance. Outcomes should be provided in a timely manner, both in writing and verbally. Complainants should sign an outcome form both to acknowledge receipt and to confirm the grievance was handled in a respectful manner. If compensation is due, the company should ensure it is made quickly.

5. The procedure, and outcomes, should be consistent

The grievance procedure must be the same for every individual who submits a grievance. The company should not expedite the process for anyone (for example, members of the local government, local contractors, or people threatening violent behavior). Outcomes must be the same for all complaints of a similar nature.

6. The procedure should include a recourse mechanism

People lodging a complaint need to have recourse if they are dissatisfied with the outcome of the investigation. Recourse mechanisms need to be local and accessible. Some companies rely on human rights commissions, an ombudsman, or other trusted bodies to provide communities with grievance recourse. A company can also establish committees or arbiters to ensure fair outcomes when there are disagreements.

Each of these attributes ensures that the grievance procedure is respectful. The grievance procedure sends a message to the community that its concerns are important to the company. If people feel that the company has a genuine interest in their problems, and a true commitment to responding to them, they will use the grievance procedure, rather than other means, to approach a company with complaints.

Indications that a grievance procedure is working

- There is a spike in the number of complaints, followed by a reduction over time.
- Demands for compensation become less strong over time.
- There is a decrease in violent or obstructive behavior.

- People say they have a venue to discuss grievances in a non-confrontational manner.

- There are fewer repeat complaints filed against the same department.

- Fewer appeals are made.

- People sign the grievance outcome form affirming that the grievance process has been respectful, even if the outcome is not in their favor.

10
Community projects

Luis was dreading this morning's staff meeting. Here he was, working for a company that genuinely wanted to contribute to local development. He ran a well-staffed department and had managed to secure a generous budget despite questions from an operations department that thought the company spent too much money on greedy communities. His managing director had given him a free hand with one proviso: his department's efforts should lead to a positive relationship between the company and the communities.

Luis had gotten to work early and found that, just last night, a local youth group had blocked a company road. This was really annoying because these youth came from a community where the company had donated a beautiful new school. The school had been welcomed by the community; unfortunately, the project had created other problems when two local contractors got into a terrible fight over which of them would get the contract to build the structure. Luis was beginning to think that the communities would turn anything into a conflict! He knew his managing director would be angry and would ask tough questions at the meeting . . .

The community projects issue

Many, perhaps most, companies invest in community projects. They build schools, clinics, and roads; they provide loans, training, and equipment. Some also have broad donation programs, supporting orphanages, churches, sports clubs, and the like. Companies expect these efforts to encourage and support positive company–community relations.

Communities expect and welcome such projects. Especially in poor areas, not serviced by the government, a company-built school or clinic represents important progress.

However, in spite of good intentions and high expectations, companies and communities are often disappointed by community project outcomes. Managers are surprised to find that the schools they built sit empty or that the loans they provided were spent rather than invested. Communities compete for benefits; they become angry when they see others receiving more. Governments come to expect that a company will maintain roads and provide local services. Communities grow dependent on a company that will leave when its business is complete.

> There is no correlation between the amount of money a company spends on community projects and the quality of its relationship with the community

There is no correlation (and sometimes even an inverse correlation!) between the amount of money companies spend on community projects and the health of company–community relations. CEP has visited communities where a company provided many community benefits and heard local people complain, "The company has never done anything for us." CEP has visited other communities where there are fewer visible company benefits, yet people speak favorably about the company's effects on their lives.

What goes wrong?

Using community projects as a risk mitigation tool can increase risk!

When companies use community projects as a risk mitigation tool, they tend to focus on communities that pose a threat. Companies then establish community projects in the areas that they judge to be most negatively impacted by corporate operations or in communities that are strategically positioned to block access roads or sabotage company assets. They focus on communities that are the most hostile and most demanding.

> ❝ Of course, we can't assist everybody and we have to make choices. From a business perspective it makes most sense to invest our money in

those areas where we have operations or where we have communities that are notorious for their difficult behavior. It is the best way to make sure our operations will not get interrupted. **

(Director external affairs of an oil company)

Local people then observe that the more difficult communities receive more community projects than peaceful ones. They wonder if they need to become difficult — in ways they do not want — in order to get their fair share of company projects. Community projects used as risk mitigation can reward and evoke violence. It can undermine a community's confidence that the distribution of company benefits will be fair, going to people who deserve them and not to people who don't.

Community projects can feed into inter-community jealousy or fragmentation

Communities are often in close touch with each other and watch each other intently. When people see that different communities are treated differently by a company, this can evoke accusations of unfairness. When different treatment seems arbitrary and is unrelated to transparent criteria, confusion and jealousy may emerge.

Community projects are used as a community compensation strategy

When companies award projects as a form of compensation for noise, dust, environmental damage, or another project consequence, they may be addressing symptoms of community dissatisfaction rather than underlying issues. Using community projects as a first response to problems means that the question of whether a project is in fact the most appropriate and effective response is often left unasked.

The price of the pieces

One company started a new project in an area with very demanding communities. The first team on the ground was the seismic department. The community refused to allow the team to conduct a seismic survey unless they promised to build an electrification project. The seismic team agreed. They provided and installed electricity poles during the three months they needed to finish their job. When the drilling department arrived, they were met with hostility; the community felt misled by the company. Instead of an electrification project, they ended up with poles! In order to be able to do their work, the drilling department promised to finalize the project but ended up doing only the wiring. This ensured peace during the period they were doing their part of the job. Next the pipeline contractor was forced to pay for a power plant before he could lay the pipelines. By the time the operations department arrived with the intent of establishing a long-term relationship, the communities had lost confidence in the company. It took the operations department several years to regain community trust. In order to do so it had to complete the electrification project at high costs.

Community projects are used to reward influential leaders

Companies always need to deal with formal and informal leaders who can influence public opinion. Such leaders can be genuinely helpful to the company because of their credibility in the community. They often clarify information to their constituencies, dispel rumors, and help the company and community reach consensus on issues. A company naturally wants to acknowledge the positive efforts of such people or, in other cases, to keep them from encouraging activities against the company.

Companies sometimes use infrastructure community projects as a way to show their appreciation to these important community representatives.

However, community members say that using infrastructure community projects to reward individuals is problematic. When the construction work for a community project is awarded to a local leader, communities have little input into the kinds of project selected and the processes of implementation. Many communities see these contracts as concealed gifts to individuals (contractors and leaders) rather than as benefits for the larger community.

Awarding a contract to show appreciation for leadership becomes, in some cases, more important to the company than the final product such as a school or a clinic. As a result, the company does not monitor quality and projects are often built to sub-standard levels to increase the contractor's profit margin. In some countries, communities are littered with non-functional buildings, and this creates frustration and anger among community members.

Companies have preconceived notions of what a community needs

One executive explained the rationale behind his company's community investment approach,

>   ** We will first give the community water and electricity, which are basic needs for any person. You do not have to sit down and talk with people

> to see their need. After we finish these projects, then we will talk with
> the community about what other things they want. "

This approach is not atypical.

When companies do not involve communities in the process of determining community projects, people feel managed rather than respected. Further, when projects are completed without community involvement, people feel no obligation to use or maintain the facilities.

Communities tell CEP that they are frequently ignored in the decision-making process surrounding community projects. They say that company staff define community needs based on their own views. Even when company staff use a participatory method to determine community preferences, communities say they can tell that the staff start with preconceived notions of what the company can do and that this steers the direction of the assessment. They say many company-sponsored community projects are, "A process of throwing expensive and useless projects at us that we never asked for."

They state that they would welcome a development approach that focuses on strengthening people's capacities: for example, by helping them start small businesses.

> " Of course we accept it if the company wants to give us potable water
> or a new clinic. If it is free, who wouldn't accept it? But that doesn't
> mean we like the company. They decided what is good for us and they
> gave the contract for the clinic to one of the most vocal leaders here to
> keep him quiet. If any NGO shows up and wants our support to protest
> against the company, we'll join them. "
>
> *(Local resident in Asian village)*

An emphasis on infrastructure projects misses other opportunities to engage with communities

Companies assume that local communities will not be satisfied unless they see direct benefits from a company's presence in the form of physical structures.

Communities note that companies define a community project in engineering terms rather than relationship terms. They say projects do not replace day-to-day stakeholder engagement. When companies use community projects as their primary engagement tool rather than as just one aspect of a broader community engagement approach, they focus on awarding contracts, monitoring agreements, and finalizing projects. They miss myriad opportunities to engage with communities through informal meetings, sports events, prompt responses to inquiries, and the like.

Most community projects are not sustainable without company support

Companies have genuinely good intentions when they provide community infrastructure. Managers are distressed when they compare the resources they take for granted to the lack of development in the areas where they operate. They want to demonstrate caring and generosity by providing these resources — healthcare and education, electricity and clean water — often free of charge.

There are different ways to renovate a clinic. A company could hire a local contractor, have its own engineers do the work, or involve the community in the project through communal labor. It is often easier and quicker for companies to use their own staff and equipment to construct a building in the community. However, when companies use their own resources to invest in community projects, communities often do not feel responsible for the final project. While the outcome may be the same — a renovated building — the degree of local ownership over the project, community cohesion, and the quality of company–community relations are all dependent on the approach the company takes.

When companies use their own resources, communities might feel less responsible for the final project

In addition, although communities appreciate a company's gesture when it builds a clinic or provides free services, they grow accustomed to having these things provided for free. If the company starts charging people for services to work toward sustainability of the project, it creates tension with the community who by that time consider it their right to have free access to these services.

Managers are sometimes surprised to learn that projects that they undertake as a part of their company's sustainable development program are in fact neither sustainable nor developmental. If a well-educated and healthy population is better informed and has more energy to initiate activities, is it not logical to assume that when corporations build schools and clinics, they are making appropriate contributions to development? There is a great deal of evidence that such projects more often result in community dependence on a company than in the basic economic growth on which sustainable development depends.

Sustainable development projects may be neither sustainable nor developmental

Where governments do not have sufficient resources or will to provide services, a company's efforts to do so can relieve the government of its responsibility. When communities come to depend on a company to provide things that their government should have provided, a company finds itself serving as a substitute for legitimate governance systems. If government cannot provide staff for a school or a clinic, the empty building serves as a reminder to local communities of unfulfilled hopes and expectations. If managers ultimately feel that they must hire doctors and teachers, they again undertake governmental functions that cannot be sustained once they leave the area.

Although the provision of services makes sense from a company perspective and provides a level of quality of services to those who lacked these services before, substitution for government functions has several serious negative consequences:

It undermines the legitimacy of governments

When companies underscore their provision of benefits to communities, it can undermine a government's legitimacy. Companies often seek recognition for what they have built by placing a sign with the corporate logo over the door. Although understandable from a company perspective, this reminds people that their government is ineffective.

It undermines government's responsibilities

When companies intervene in the areas of public infrastructure, it can weaken processes by which citizens hold their government accountable. CEP has met government officials who, upon seeing that corporations are willing to provide infrastructure, instruct communities to go to the company to get what they want. Some governments come to expect that if they do not provide services, companies will be compelled to provide them. Such an attitude can also be found among opposition or rebel groups who have told outsiders, "If the company will take care of the population, we (the rebel force) will take care of the fighting."

It causes conflict after the company leaves

Companies typically support the provision of high-quality services in the areas where they work. Continuing to provide this quality of services after the company leaves is often beyond the capacity of even a willing government. Without an exit strategy as part of the design at the start of a program, companies assume they will hand over the hospital or clinic to the government. The government may never be ready to assume these projects because they do not have the means or because they feel the area where a company has provided services has already benefited enough that government resources should help people in other areas.

It reinforces dependency

When companies provide services that should be provided by the government, communities increasingly turn to and rely on companies to meet their needs. In some cases, companies have provided piped water, electricity, roads, education, and many other benefits for over 40 years! One community was very upset when they were required to start paying a consultation fee in a company-supported clinic even though this was common practice in all other areas of the country.

It frees money for governments to conduct warfare

Corporations sometimes establish social service systems for communities where they want peaceful relations in the midst of broader conflict. These systems can substitute for supports that would ordinarily have been supplied by community leaders or government. This allows the government's resources to be used for the pursuit of warfare.

Donation programs often create dissatisfaction with the company

Companies make donations to local charities and other worthy causes as a part of their corporate citizenship. They provide school uniforms and scholarships, support orphanages, provide gifts or holidays, provide relief goods if there is a disaster, and so on. Companies also set up company-resourced grants programs as a mechanism for responding to small funding requests from local community groups.

People who receive these donations and grants appreciate them. However, experience shows these gifts do not create an overall positive community attitude toward a company and very often backfire by raising expectations that cannot be met.

In one place, the community relations officers in charge of the company donation program reported that they spent close to 40% of their time simply following up on requests for donations and verifying that the requests were for real need. They felt that this time could have been better spent interacting with a broad number of people on issues of general community concern. In this same location, community people complained that the company's program favored the elites who knew how to work the system.

If only 25% of the request for donations can be awarded, 75% will be disappointed

In another area, staff reported that they received over 200 requests every year and that they awarded funding to about 25% of these. This meant that three-quarters of the people who requested support were inevitably disappointed. These staff were overwhelmed with so many requests. They believed that their program was a generous one since they responded positively to 50 requests every year; however, local people complained. Upon reflection, it was not surprising that turning down 150 requests each year would lead to widespread disappointment. Further, community people said they did not understand why some proposals received funding and others did not. They said, "We don't ask for a donation very often." People complained that they did not receive feedback on their proposals so they never knew why their requests were turned down. The selection criteria were not clear or transparent, and they were seen as unfair. People said a lottery might have been fairer!

Company–NGO partnerships do not always improve company–community relations

Increasingly, companies are developing partnerships with service NGOs to facilitate the companies' community relations programs. Corporate managers assume that NGOs are always able to gain the trust of communities and develop cordial relations with them that will ensure a favorable relationship for the company as well. The evidence on this, however, is mixed.

Communities say that sometimes companies choose the *wrong* NGOs to work with them and this worsens community relations. Communities have no respect for what they call "pocket NGOs" or "briefcase NGOs." These are operations that have been created by one or two people who claim to be establishing an NGO but, in fact, who are positioning themselves to obtain personal funding, prestige and/or power through association with companies. In areas where a corporation experiences community unrest and dissatisfaction, we have seen corporate managers accept at face value well-spoken individuals who present themselves in the corporate office, claim to represent a community, and offer to help by partnering with the corporation to address community concerns. While some of these individuals may genuinely want to improve community life, more often they are taking advantage of the corporate need to find some way to relate to local people.

Some corporations create an NGO to carry out their community-based work. The assumption is that they can fund and develop an NGO with the right skills and qualities to do good and trusted work. Experience shows that this approach can backfire. One community complained vigorously to CEP that the company manager created an NGO, staffed it with people he chose, and then proceeded to carry out so-called development projects that he deemed important rather than those that the community sought. In many places, CEP hears people speak of the "company's NGO" with disdain, noting that it is "only window dressing" or "only here to buy community favor." Further, when a company develops its own NGO, this sends a signal to all other NGOs and community people that the existing structures are not trusted or qualified.

Corporations also err when they expect too much from NGO partnerships. CEP has heard company managers describe their NGO relationship as if it will provide a permanent license to operate in the communities serviced by the NGO. However, even the best NGO–community program that can be imagined cannot buy community acceptance of a corporation. It cannot substitute for healthy direct corporate–community interactions (as many of the sections of this book show).

'It would have been *our* bridge'

One company established a local NGO to engage in community development activities. The NGO decided to build a walking bridge across a ravine that divided people from markets. Local villagers claimed that they did not support this decision. The project created conflict between the community and the NGO over allegations of corruption. The community became upset that the company set up an NGO to spend "their" money on a project decided without their involvement.

When asked later what local villagers would do with the money had the company made it available to them they said, "We might have used the money to build the same bridge, but it would have been *our* bridge because we would have been involved in the decision-making process. Now it is the company's bridge and we don't like it."

Options for getting it right

Companies feel they have a responsibility to ensure that their presence generates tangible benefits to local communities. However, they should recognize that they are not development agencies. Further, they need to acknowledge that all the inter-governmental, NGO, and international institutional support for sustainable development has, as yet, not brought full-scale economic growth to most societies where it has been offered. Recognizing past mistakes and limits to sustainable development efforts, and acknowledging the complex mix of economic and political factors involved in true sustainable development, is an important first step that companies must take to **get it right** with regard to community projects.

Clarify company goals, the strategy to achieve them, and the link to the business case

Community projects should be approached with the same rigor and professionalism applied to all other aspects of corporate operations. Companies should determine clear objectives for any community project efforts and design a strategy, linked to the business case, for achieving the objectives.

In some contexts, staff feel pressured to accept proposals from important community leaders or others such as the general manager's spouse. Being able to refer to a business process helps ensure that programs are aligned with the corporate objectives and serves as a useful tool for field staff to shield themselves from pressure. Clarity on goals and strategies also provides clarity about what communities can and cannot expect and reduces the likelihood that social investment programs will lead to jealousy between groups that arise from non-transparent decision-making criteria.

When communities know what to expect from companies, the likelihood of jealousy is reduced

Leverage corporate connections and access to address local needs

An increasing number of companies use their access to governments and their financial leverage to promote education and health in areas where they operate. Recognizing the dangers of substituting for government, they act as a catalyst for ensuring community needs are met.

Using leverage to attract external donor funds

One company found an international donor to fund the construction of a building to house different law enforcement agencies. With this funding in hand, the company was able to get the national government to agree to provide salaries and to handle maintenance of the building. The company provided only furniture. Local residents emphasized the role of the company in lobbying donor agencies and the government to establish the facility and to increase law enforcement mechanisms benefiting local communities. Without the company, communities said, the project would not have happened.

Using leverage to lobby the government

Local officials demanded kickbacks from landowners before they would pay out land compensation. Landowners felt powerless. When the company heard about this, it contacted the President's office to ensure that the correct amounts were paid without bribes.

Other companies have exercised a convening power to bring government representatives and local communities together to discuss steps toward ensuring government-provided services. This process provided everything a company might have done, but avoided the dependency on company funding. The point is for com-

Companies must move away from doing it themselves to making sure it gets done

panies to move away from doing it themselves to making sure it gets done by the appropriate agencies.

Take a tripartite approach

Another form of leverage used by an increasing number of companies involves a tripartite partnership model between the company, the government, and local communities. Each of the three partners contributes to making a project successful. If building a bridge, the government may provide materials, the company technical advice, and the community the labor. Advantages of this model include increased accountability and legitimacy of the government, community ownership of outcomes, and decreased dependency on the company.

Sometimes, communities and authorities are quick to agree to a tripartite approach but then lack the persistence to complete the project. Companies who have used this approach note the importance of having a solid agreement and good understanding about the roles and responsibilities of each party. Many rely on jointly developed memoranda of understanding.

In cases where several parties agree to make a financial contribution, some companies have established a trust fund and have not begun any construction work on the project until all parties have made their contributions. This reduces the possibility that the company is the only party to provide funds.

One company's tripartite approach to infrastructure projects

Objectives

- To increase the legitimacy of local authorities. Local authorities, not the company are seen to be in control.

Company conditions

- Financial contributions from each party made before the project commences

Approach

- Construction is phased: crews focus on completing one part of the project at a time to gain momentum, build on success, and ensure minimal clean-up in case the project was interrupted.

Focus on the process of determining and implementing community projects

Processes by which community projects are implemented are as important as the final project result in determining how a community feels about a company. Companies are becoming increasingly aware of the importance of community consultation and the provision of training (financial management, business development, etc.) as parts of their community project development. They are moving away from traditional charity or the unconditional provision of infrastructure projects.

> Spending more money on community projects does not guarantee a more successful outcome

The extent of community involvement in the decision making and implementation of the project determines the long-term success of community projects. It is also important for communities with differing priorities to reach agreements about types of project and methods for achieving them. Helping communities that start from different places come to agreement benefits communities and community–company relations.

Some companies successfully use traditional infrastructure projects as a means to help people organize themselves, build consensus, and strengthen their organizational capacities. The case study below describes an example of this.

Using infrastructure projects to bring communities together

One company saw its activities hampered by a community. Local youth did not recognize the traditional leadership structure. As a result the community was fragmented and leaderless. The company decided to use a community project – renovating a school – to provide a tangible benefit *and* a means of bringing people together. It designed the process of selecting and implementing the community project so that all sub-groups (youth, elders, women) had to sit together and agree on how they would implement the project. The company's objective was to ensure that local community members felt involved in the decision-making process and in the implementation of the project and that they took ownership for the completion and maintenance of the project. Although the company had plenty of resources to hire a contractor and to build a new school, by emphasizing the process the company encouraged new community-wide forms of consultation and decision making. Community members reported that, if it were not for the company, they would never have been able to work together and to complete the school renovation project.

In the case of a small grants program, companies have hired an NGO to help people write proposals for funding, seek alternative funding sources, or design a structured business plan.

Ask local communities how community projects fit into their future

An effective and often overlooked approach for developing community projects is
to ask local communities how they see their own future. Company-aided community projects should always connect to and support communities in their own
efforts to reach their long-term aspirations. Independent outside NGOs or facilita-
tors that enjoy credibility can conduct assessments by using a participatory rural
appraisal (PRA) to determine the aspirations of the community and to prioritize
these based on available resources. To the surprise of many managers − who
expected that a PRA would produce a shopping list of requests for schools and clinics − communities often prioritize training and strengthening of soft skills if they
know a company is prepared to support them over a longer period of time. Some
companies assist local communities (often through NGOs) in designing a longer-
term development plan. This development plan can also help the community to
solicit support from donors other than the company, provided the company helps
the community set reasonable expectations and reachable goals.

Benefits related to the company's core processes should be considered legitimate community investment efforts

Helping local people qualify for and obtain contracts with a company, providing
support to local entrepreneurs in getting a bank loan, or training young people to
draft a business plan are all legitimate community development efforts. One company encourages its employees to share their experiences in seminars on accounting, project management, and other aspects of their work with businesses and civic
groups. Such activities may increase the quality and quantity of a local community's
representation in the company's workforce and contractor pool. Chapter 8 dis-
cusses other aspects of such local content in more detail.

Some rules of thumb to ensure that community projects are sustainable[4]

Many companies recognize that projects should be able to function successfully without their ongoing support. In reality, many community projects we have seen would cease to exist if the company were to leave an area. Figure 10.1 shows the company approach needed to shift a community's position from dependence to development. To support sustainability of community projects (which is not the same as long-term sustainable development) companies should:

- **Make sure that a company exit strategy is part of the design of any new community project.**

- **Build on existing plans, assets, and capacities.** For example, renovate existing school buildings rather than build new ones. Existing schools have teachers, furniture, and equipment, but the government may not be able to guarantee these supplies to new structures. Or make a point to follow and fit into, rather than to duplicate or add to, existing government development plans.

- **Recognize the responsibility of communities for their own success.** One sustainable development expert stated, "Dependency starts when you have a lack of confidence in the communities' ability to achieve things." Communities know that, if they wait long enough, the company will do what is needed. Companies need to resist the impulse to take the initiative for community projects if communities themselves do not.

- **Help people recognize the importance of making choices and setting priorities.** Communities can make unlimited requests to a company without having any discussion about priorities. If communities are provided with a specified budget for community projects, this can facilitate a discussion of priorities and ensure that people figure out how to use funds to achieve the greatest possible benefit among alternatives.

- **Obtain community or government commitment to maintain a completed project.** Many companies now make community projects conditional on how the community has maintained previous projects. For example, a community may establish a water and sanitation committee to

---

4   CEP has drafted a more elaborate guidance document for the oil and gas industry on social investment projects: Luc Zandvliet, *Guide to Successful Sustainable Social Investment for the Oil and Gas Industry* (London: International Petroleum Industry Environmental Conservation Association, Social Responsibility Working Group, 2008; www.ipieca.org).

Figure 10.1 **From dependency to development**

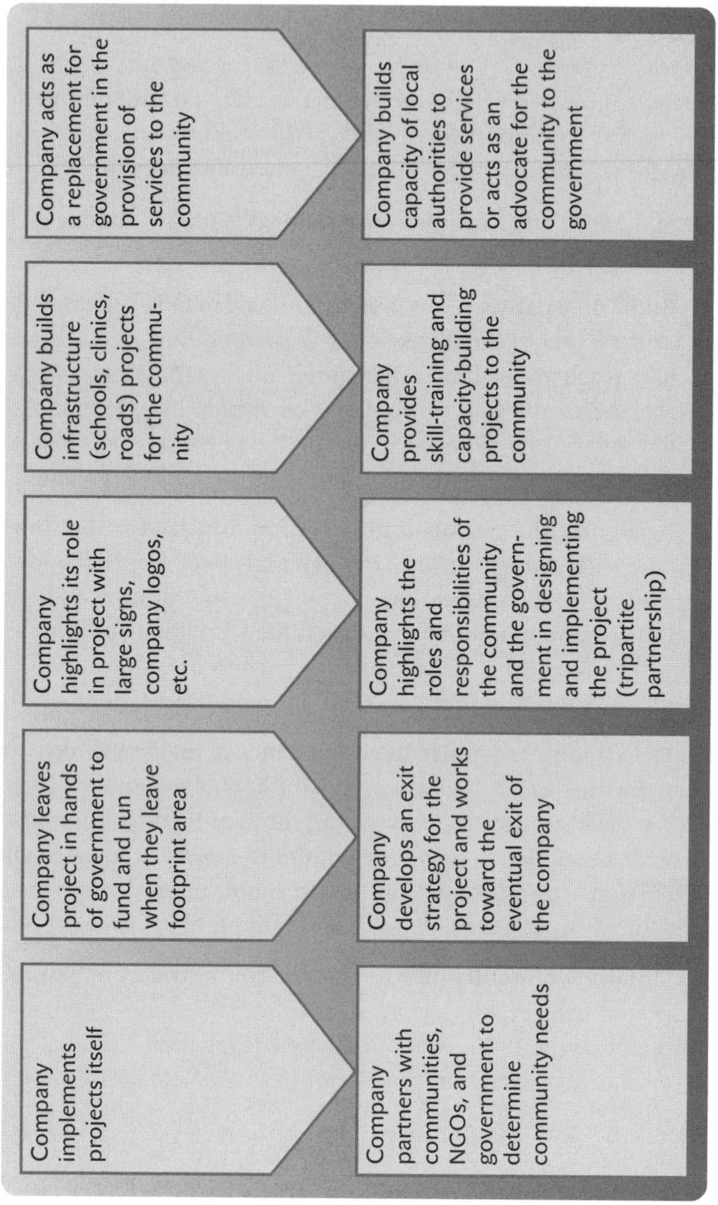

Company implements projects itself	Company leaves project in hands of government to fund and run when they leave footprint area	Company highlights its role in project with large signs, company logos, etc.	Company builds infrastructure (schools, clinics, roads) projects for the community	Company acts as a replacement for government in the provision of services to the community
Company partners with communities, NGOs, and government to determine community needs	Company develops an exit strategy for the project and works toward the eventual exit of the company	Company highlights the roles and responsibilities of the community and the government in designing and implementing the project (tripartite partnership)	Company provides skill-training and capacity-building projects to the community	Company builds capacity of local authorities to provide services or acts as an advocate for the community to the government

collect user fees for maintenance. To ensure that communities have the capacity to maintain any planned project, community projects can include a training component on facilities maintenance, project management, or other skills that enable the communities to run their own projects without dependency on the company.

- **Do not provide free services.** Experience shows that handouts and free services gain temporary, but not permanent, goodwill from communities. Working *with* people rather than *for* them to set priorities evokes discussion about which projects are worth community effort. Because people are generally busy before any community project is launched, choices they will make about involvement in building or maintaining a project will be weighed against their opportunity costs. What else would they have done with this time or money if they had not undertaken this particular community project with the company? People have to make choices and set priorities about which projects deserve their time and resources.

Indicators of effective community projects

- Communities say their quality of life is better.
- Communities say the government is more accountable and more responsive as a result of the company's approach.
- Company-sponsored projects are sustainable and effective without company support.
- Communities attribute increased collaboration between sub-groups to the approach taken by the company.
- Communities increasingly invest more of their own resources (money, labor) in community projects.
- Communities request soft skills support more than material support.
- There is no conflict between communities, or within communities, about getting access to social investment projects.

11
Working with advocacy NGOs

Charlie, the president of a large, multinational corporation met with his senior management team. He complained, "We are completely powerless with the NGOs! They claim the moral high ground and, when we try to respond, we only appear defensive. Their agenda is to create trouble for the company, and there is nothing we can do. There is nothing we can do!"

The number of NGOs and the range of issues they embrace are growing. In some relatively small countries where CEP has visited corporate operations, there have been more than 300 local NGOs. Many of these local NGOs are connected to and supported by international NGOs. They are often staffed by people who have been educated in European or North American universities who are articulate, professional, and strongly committed to positive social change.

NGOs with similar interests are increasingly connected. In some quite remote areas, we have seen small, locally based NGOs using the Internet to learn about environmental or human rights issues, corporate codes of conduct, and a company's history of compliance or non-compliance with international standards, and to learn how to organize anti-corporate campaigns and to elicit support for their causes.

That there are more NGOs operating at more levels and becoming better organized and increasingly connected internationally is now a fact of life for corporations. NGO interest in corporate operations is a new and growing challenge for international companies.

Importantly, there are many types of NGO with different interests, modes of operation, purposes, and motivations. When managers assume that all NGOs are alike, they are not able to take advantage of the knowledge and opportunities that some offer, and they fail to recognize the potential dangers and traps that others pose. Some NGOs are honorable; some are not. Some are well managed and some not. Some are large with multiple international branches (although not as powerful as most corporate managers seem to assume). Some have a large membership on whose behalf they speak; others lack broad public support. Within any single NGO, operational competence and styles of interaction of the staff or of different departments also vary. Recognition of interagency and intra-agency variations is important in responding to any NGO.

Corporate managers need to recognize that there are two broad types of NGO: service NGOs, such as humanitarian aid or development assistance; and advocacy NGOs, which attempt to influence public opinion (and corporate behavior) on issues of indigenous rights, human rights, the environment, or the political situation of a specific country. In recent years a number of development NGOs have developed advocacy departments and thus perform both a service and an advocacy function. Some NGOs work with companies (and accept their money), whereas others feel that close association with corporations taints their activities.

> There are many types of NGO with different interests, modes of operation, purposes, and motivations

The NGOs that fall within the two broad categories have different objectives and mandates. They require different approaches for engagement. This chapter focuses on a company's relationships with advocacy NGOs. Working with service NGOs is discussed in Chapter 10.

The advocacy NGO issue

CEP has seen a number of senior managers of large and powerful corporations become unnerved by advocacy NGOs. An encounter with an NGO often elicits a corporate response that is poorly thought out and more concerned with public relations and corporate image than with engaging to correct mistakes.

Such unproductive responses often have a history. Many company executives describe unpleasant encounters with NGOs. One senior manager told of his first attempt to reach out to a group of critical NGOs in his region. He asked for a meeting and arrived at the agreed time. However, rather than engaging with him in conversation, the NGO director simply harangued the company. When the corporate manager tried to signal that he was there to address problematic issues, the NGO

Figure 11.1 **Spot the differences?**

Companies talking about NGOs	NGOs talking about companies
"**They are not accountable to anybody**, while we are held accountable by our shareholders, customers, and other stakeholders."	"**They are not accountable to anybody**. Institutions such as the WTO or the ICC are non-elected bodies that only serve to further the corporate agenda."
"**They are powerful**. You cannot win the debate even if you are right since they are trusted by society and the media."	"**They are powerful**. They have the means to influence politics and hire the best lawyers to defend their interests."
"They use us as proxy targets to **further their own agendas**, such as the anti-globalization agenda."	"They only **further their own corporate agenda** of increasing profits, no matter what social face they put on."
"**You cannot change or influence them** since they feel they are morally right."	"**You cannot change them** since they believe nobody can tell them what to do or how to do it."

ICC, International Chamber of Commerce; WTO, World Trade Organization

representative showed no interest in helping the company change. We have heard of a number of such encounters where corporate managers have been frustrated and insulted by the apparent intransigence and rudeness of NGO people. Encounters like this convince company staff that NGOs are more interested in attacking corporations than they are in effecting positive changes in corporate behavior.

We hear similar stories from NGO colleagues who report that their genuine attempts to engage with corporate managers have been met with suspicion, arrogance, hostility, and long-winded "explanations" about how little they understand about the real world. They find the downputting and mistrustful posturing by company executives insulting.

In fact, CEP finds that companies and advocacy NGOs very often accuse each other of exactly the same things as shown in the examples in Figure 11.1.

What goes wrong?

Companies think advocacy NGOs offer criticisms not solutions

Corporate managers often assume that advocacy NGOs are well-organized and well-financed adversaries whose sole interest is in making the company look bad. When these assumptions are present, corporate managers act beleaguered and defensive, thereby evoking even more criticism. As adversarial positions escalate, managers see NGOs, in their words, as "so extreme that there is no point in engaging with them."

Advocacy groups say that it is not their duty to provide solutions for companies. Their role is to raise concerns about negative impacts they see coming from corporate activities. They also note that someone needs to represent those who have little or no voice – such as local communities or the environment – to counterbalance immense corporate power.

> When a manager interprets all advocacy actions through a negative lens, opportunities for developing new options are lost

When companies and NGOs interpret each other through a negative lens, assuming trickery, dishonesty, and ill will, opportunities for engagement that would develop positive options are lost. Accused of ill will, corporations become ever-more committed to an anti-NGO position. And, when they are accused of ill will, NGOs become ever-more committed to an anti-corporation position. The result is failed communication and entrenched positions. Local communities suffer.

On – and off – the record

Although his public stance was for corporate divestment from a given country, a well-known anti-corporate activist suggested to a CEP team that a company would benefit local people by encouraging additional corporate investment in that country. His off-the-record argument was that additional international influence could bring both economic and political benefits.

When he heard this suggestion, the corporate manager did not trust it. He was unable to believe that the activist who had caused his company so much trouble could genuinely acknowledge possible positive impacts of international investment. What could have been an opening for the NGO and company to explore corporate options together was lost because of a history of mistrust.

Companies think NGOs have unrealistic expectations and demands

Companies assume that advocacy groups expect them to make everything right — bringing peace to war-torn countries or eliminating human rights violations by oppressive host-country governments. Unable to live up to these expectations, they often see no point in engaging with advocacy groups around these issues.

In reality, the majority of NGOs know that such expectations are unrealistic for corporations. Instead, they want companies to acknowledge difficulties and be transparent about what they are doing to provide a positive influence in relation to large problems. Thinking expectations are too high, company managers often resort to glossy reports and slick websites which describe only positive impacts and never acknowledge dilemmas and difficulties. Not surprisingly, advocacy NGOs are put off by public relations responses to real suffering and, as a result, intensify their campaigns against companies who, they say, "Are only interested in profits, not people's welfare."

Some NGOs distort facts to make political points

Some advocacy NGOs focus their efforts on a single issue, a single company, or even a particular site of a company. Sometimes these NGOs effectively become the authorities on the area of their focus and are cited by other organizations that base their own campaigns on information obtained from these expert NGOs. This is problematic when the expert NGO provides information that is not accurate. In the face of campaigns based on what they believe to be lies, corporate managers become angry and dismissive rather than focused on improving their practice.

Corporations fear public exposure

Again because of history, companies fear lawsuits, shareholder challenges, and consumer demonstrations. Legal processes, initiated in either host or home countries, have sometimes dragged on for years at high costs to corporations in terms of money and public image. Shareholder challenges and consumer boycotts also raise the negative public profile of companies and cost time and money. Knowledge that advocacy NGOs can organize these kinds of anti-company action affects the thinking of many corporate executives whenever their companies are approached by an NGO.

Corporate managers question the legitimacy of advocacy NGOs

Some company managers see NGO campaigns as driven more by the political interests of people in the North than by the interests of people of the poorer countries where companies operate. They think it inappropriate that relatively wealthy individuals from Europe and North America take on the causes of local people in remote areas. They question claims that Northern NGOs can empower local people.

When an NGO has no local presence, managers question whether it has a real mandate to speak on behalf of local communities. Managers question the legitimacy of other local groups which call themselves NGOs but which, in fact, simply make money by threatening violence or by ostensibly linking to an external cause to receive international funding. However, when managers question the motive or legitimacy of an NGO, they also tend to dismiss any issues that the NGO brings to their attention, often without determining whether or not the issue has substance or enjoys public support.

For their part, communities say that they support advocacy groups mainly because, in their words, "It is our only way to influence company decisions." NGOs are seen as one of the few ways that communities can communicate ideas and raise problems with corporations without violence. When managers ignore this, they miss one opportunity for avoiding violent confrontations with communities. When communities see that a company only reacts defensively, it reinforces their sense that the company is rigid and arrogant so they need a powerful third party, such as an NGO, to help them be heard.

Options for getting it right

Recognize that NGOs often raise issues that need to be addressed

Issues that concern advocacy NGOs do not appear suddenly from nowhere. It takes time for an NGO to identify a problem, garner interest and support around it, and approach a company with its concerns. It takes time for an NGO to develop sufficient funding and strength to challenge a company — especially with legal action in court.

Companies need to realize that NGOs, particularly those with large memberships, cannot exist without public support. They represent, at least in part, changing societal values and expectations with regard to company operations. Many NGOs have real expertise in researching problems, disentangling and clarifying their components, articulating and educating about them, achieving legislation to correct them, and monitoring progress on solving them. They deserve credit for this expertise. Constructive engagement with such NGOs becomes a strategy to align business interests with societal expectations.

Recognizing that there is a significant lead time before negative campaigns gain public momentum and recognizing that NGOs have expertise in important areas, companies could welcome NGOs (even challenging NGOs) as allies for addressing issues before they become intractable. Even when NGOs do not want to work with a company, their advocacy can provide an early warning system to alert companies to potential destabilizing problems.

Recognize that local communities work with people who are most likely to solve problems

Across contexts, communities indicate they support advocacy groups only when they feel that they get a better deal doing so than they get by working with the company. Companies and advocacy groups are, in a sense, in competition for the favor of local communities, and advocacy NGOs can be effective only if the company fails in its engagement with local communities. This reality gives companies a great deal of control over how effective outside critics can become. It also means that, when advocacy groups arrive in the footprint area of a company, it should signal managers to closely examine the quality of their relations with local people.

> Advocacy NGOs can be effective only if the company has failed in its engagement with local communities

When companies engage with advocacy groups as a last resort, they react to the manifestations rather than the causes of grievances. They will have already lost control over the outcome of company–NGO interactions.

Using violence to attract international attention

Staff of a local NGO, previously ignored by a company, proudly explained how they had managed to get the company to listen to them. They had first sent letters to the company demanding that more local people be employed, but, when the company did not respond, they blocked the company gates. They knew the company could not accept this. As expected, the company called police in to break up the peaceful protest; shots were fired and six people suffered bullet wounds. The next day, websites around the world published the story of this protest and the company's response. NGO staff celebrated their victory and observed, "We would have received no attention had this remained a labor issue. But the shooting made it a human rights issue. Now we have so much attention that the company has to listen to us."

Develop a mechanism for listening to the local voices that NGOs claim to represent

Although international criticisms of a company often contain elements of truth, at times they do not correspond with local perceptions. Even when local communities are satisfied with a corporation's performance, they often do not have a platform from which to be heard internationally. Many of the efforts and positive impacts of companies go unseen because there are no credible groups of local people who can organize themselves and articulate their views the way an advocacy group can. In practice, this means that, when a journalist visits a country or site, the negative impacts of the corporate presence are better explained than the positive impacts.

Companies can and should develop systems by which they regularly hear from local constituencies and can demonstrate that they are listening and responding to local opinion. Some companies systematically document attendees' names at weekly farmers', women's, or youth meetings, record questions asked and responses provided, and track the issues that are raised and the solutions that are agreed to. These data are maintained on a daily basis. Although not primarily intended to counter allegations from advocacy NGOs, such a system provides a company with a good sense of local perceptions and provides a basis on which to counter assertions made by outsiders when these are factually incorrect.

Some companies engage outside NGOs or university groups to help communities better articulate their own ideas and perceptions and develop negotiation and communication skills. When community members feel strong in their own ability to speak out and to negotiate around problems, they do not need an outside advocacy NGO to speak on their behalf. In some places local communities have asked outside advocacy groups to leave when they see that they do not speak on behalf of the community.

When companies actively build local constituencies that are articulate and able to provide their side of the story as effectively as (international) NGOs can, this increases the probability that local people's opinions will lead (rather than be submerged by) international campaigns. Careful and regular company–community engagement is the basis by which a company can show the outside world that company staff know at least as much about local perceptions as outside advocacy NGOs know. This can counter an NGO's claim to speak on behalf of local communities. Further, such mechanisms also reinforce local communities' sense that they are respected and trusted.

Focus on the objectives that companies and advocacy groups share

Although companies and advocacy groups have different agendas, they also share many objectives. Both want to increase the capacity and willingness of local authorities to be accountable and responsive to the needs of their people. Both want to ensure that human rights are protected. Both want to promote social and economic development. Rather than focusing on how they differ from NGOs, companies could emphasize areas of mutual concern and build on these as opportunities for constructive engagement.

Recognize that there are different types of advocacy NGO

Not all advocacy groups are anti-corporation. In each of the situations where CEP has worked, we have found wide-ranging differences of opinion and strategy among the advocacy NGOs. While some take strong public anti-corporate positions, others are keen to work with companies on transparency, human rights, environmental preservation, development, and humanitarian action.

Reach out to and work with advocacy groups who are willing

When companies seek partnerships with groups that are willing to work with them, this can have the additional impact of reducing space for more extreme claims. NGOs monitor each other and, if one steps out of line in terms of vitriol, others are able to respond with their point of view. When a company is seen to be working effectively with groups that are willing to be part of the solution, those who are single-mindedly critical of companies will find it increasingly difficult to be taken seriously in the public arena.

NGOs and accountability

In one case, NGOs who were part of a round table asked a company to stop a certain activity and the company agreed to do so. Complicated logistics meant it took the company some months to implement this change. One NGO wanted to embark on a public campaign to pressure the company to speed up its procedure. When another NGO learned about this, it successfully insisted that the first NGO halt its campaign and acknowledge the company's constructive efforts.

Involve NGOs from the start of company activities

Discussing challenges, dilemmas, or positive impacts with outside groups before a crisis allows such stakeholders to perform due diligence *before* a company becomes subjected to campaigns. When a company highlights its positive efforts only after a campaign has already been launched against it, it loses credibility and allows critics to easily dismiss those efforts as a cover-up.

Invite advocacy groups to help set company standards and audit company policies, practices, and impacts

Some companies establish working relations with specific agencies — for example, environmental or human rights groups — to set reasonable standards for company processes. Some also agree with local or international NGOs to monitor and publicize community impacts of company operations. One corporate vice president whose company was developing this kind of arrangement with a human rights NGO told us that he saw this as insurance against future lawsuits. If his company were attentive to human rights concerns from the beginning of its operations and were seen by advocacy NGOs to be taking steps to monitor all impacts, the probability of a later lawsuit alleging violations would be reduced. He noted that he believed his company's impacts to be positive (or at least not negative) and wanted the partner NGO to publicize this to the world. But he acknowledged that, if the NGO found problems, he would rather know and be able to correct them early than to find out about them later and be (rightly) held accountable for them when he could have prevented them.

Establish formal structures for company–NGO engagement

Some companies have included members of NGOs in their governance structures such as the Board of Directors or on specific advisory boards. These moves are credible only when the company takes seriously the suggestions and recommendations made by NGO members.

Some companies engage with a group of select advocacy NGOs on a periodic basis (e.g., twice a year). Companies are represented at these meetings by senior managers who are in a position to make decisions. The agendas are designed by the NGOs. Managers and NGO representatives say such regular discussions offer the following advantages:

- Lend credibility to the company's intention to engage constructively with critics.

- Give the company a face in the eyes of the NGOs.

- Reassure NGOs that they have the company's attention so they do not feel their only avenue for affecting corporate behavior is through lawsuits or the media.

- Provide a venue for development of personal relationships that over time can be relied on for informal communication to verify rumors or exchange facts.

- Legitimize the constructive and moderate activists groups, thereby reducing the space for radical and non-constructive operations.

- Give space for NGOs that are part of the group to hold each other accountable.

Work toward agreement on disputed facts

When parties agree on the basic facts of issues, it becomes possible to find solutions to problems. Agreement on facts supports discussion of how the facts should be interpreted and how they can be addressed. Companies can help advocacy NGOs gather facts, and ensure they are accurate, by inviting them, or the press, to visit operational sites to observe and hear what local people say. Openness to investigation and joint fact-finding missions can cut through emotional differences and focus discussions on constructive solutions. One advantage of inviting multiple agencies to visit corporate sites is that this allows them to correct each other's information.

Be transparent about corporate procedures for dealing with difficult issues

Many companies have elaborate procedures in place related to CSR issues such as environmental accidents or allegations of human rights abuses. They collect information, analyze its accuracy, and engage with authorities to take action. Often such procedures are not public so they go unnoticed by the outside world. Being more explicit about the processes in place, the occasions on which action is undertaken, and the company's accomplishments can contribute to a more accurate understanding of the company's policies and activities. Not being open and clear about these allows the outside world to assume that a company does nothing to address issues of concern.

Work with NGOs to establish goals for the company

Advocacy NGOs are good at identifying and voicing problems, but often less good at offering solutions. If a company can get advocacy NGOs to work with them to specify appropriate benchmarks of improvement, then both can agree on how to monitor results of company efforts. Getting to agreement on benchmarks can be a useful first step in recognizing where company and NGOs share objectives. Benchmark discussions can also include agreement on criteria by which progress (or failure to progress) will be assessed, and this can help the two parties come to a fuller understanding of appropriate corporate roles in influencing broader social justice.

Clarify who is speaking on whose behalf

Many but not all advocacy groups operate in a professional manner on behalf of their constituencies. It is always important to verify the credibility and mandates of NGOs when they claim to speak on behalf of the local people. One easy but often overlooked way to check credibility is to ask communities who they see as their representatives and to what extent they support an advocacy group. Some companies always engage with advocacy NGOs in public view of local communities. This way, people can hear what is being said and can immediately hold both NGO and company accountable. If an NGO makes claims that are not supported by local communities, this becomes clear to everyone immediately.

> ❝ It is easy for people in London or Washington to tell the world what should happen in this country. But they are rich and safe, while our main concern is how we can get two meals a day for our families. We do not care about politics; we just want a better life no matter which type of leader is in charge. ❞
>
> *(Farmer in a politically oppressed country)*

International NGOs, national NGOs, and communities are not always on the same page!

The agendas of international NGOs, national NGOs, and local communities are often different and even contradictory. In one country, a mining company used a nearby river for its mine tailings. The international NGOs objected to this practice, quoting international standards and arguing that the company should immediately halt operations if no alternative disposal system could be found. The national NGOs wanted to have serious discussions with the company about how it could alter its practices to diminish waste disposal. They did not want the company to halt operations because they were worried about the loss of jobs if mining stopped. The community that lived downstream where the pollution effects were felt disagreed with all the NGOs, saying, "We absolutely do not want this practice to end. Of course we suffer, but as long as the company compensates us with a clinic or a school building, we accept it. This is our only chance to get these kinds of benefits!"

Focus on process rather than outcome

Most industry watchers including advocacy NGOs realize there are no easy answers to working in complex social and political environments. Recognizing this and taking responsibility to address difficult issues, some companies have started to be transparent about the dilemmas they face working in certain areas. Rather than papering over problems with glossy claims, they display a more humble tone in their publicity. They open up their websites for interactive comments, recognizing that many researchers of advocacy NGOs are young and make extensive use of the Internet. They invite ideas, suggestions, and feedback that generate options for companies to become more forward-looking.

When companies regard all advocacy NGOs as enemies, they miss out on opportunities to solve legitimate problems the NGOs may point out. When communities see companies stonewalling an NGO with broad public support, they perceive the company as arrogant and uncaring. This also gives more legitimacy to the NGO. Taking an engaged — rather than confrontational — approach is important, no matter how much the company and the NGO disagree. This type of approach sends the message that companies know they do not have all the answers but are working hard to address important issues. Some companies also give credit to advocacy NGOs, acknowledging their positive influence on corporate behavior. Some have even noted in their annual report that they learned from external pressure. When companies acknowledge NGOs' contributions and work *with* them to address problems in the community, NGOs will realize they do not have to push the company to be heard or to respond.

A balanced and transparent approach to communicating with outsiders signals that companies are serious about their social impacts and increases external ownership of solutions to difficult dilemmas.

Indicators of positive relationship with advocacy NGOs

- People say that hard-line advocacy NGOs do not speak on their behalf.
- Community members, not NGOs, are quoted in news articles voicing community perceptions.
- The company is invited by moderate advocacy groups to attend NGO meetings or workshops.
- NGOs accept company invitations to participate in meetings.
- Credible NGOs ask to work with the company.
- NGOs start to hold one another accountable for incorrect information about the company.

- NGOs publicly acknowledge that the company is trying to address issues of concern.

- NGOs start using the company's best practices as examples in their discussions with other companies.

12
Working with governments

The vice president of an international corporation with operations in many countries complained, "I just don't get it. Only ten years ago, NGOs were on our backs to respect the sovereignty of governments. They rightly pointed out that it is inappropriate for international corporations to exercise undue influence on national policies in the countries where we work. But now the NGOs want us to take responsibility for ensuring that governments in those countries respect human rights and enforce environmental standards, and they are holding us accountable for violations by those governments! Just when we learned the importance of political non-interference, they now want us to interfere!"

The government relations issue

Company managers want to get it right in their dealings with host governments. They are distressed by human rights abuse and environmental damage and would like to see governments that are stable, democratic, and accountable. They know that their companies expect them to manage these interactions so that they do not become a problem, but they have no company protocols or practical guidelines for how to ensure they succeed. They need to interact with authorities with sufficient cordiality to ensure their operations run smoothly, while maintaining sufficient distance to avoid the attention — and criticism — of the advocacy NGOs that challenge these authorities. As a result, many claim to be powerless in relation to national governments. They disavow government connections and disclaim access to government decision makers, complaining, "NGOs think we have much more power than we actually have!"

Corporate headquarters often deal with the pressures their field managers face by referring them to corporate codes of conduct and international standards. However, these are usually stated in general terms that do not provide real, clear, field-level guidance for day-to-day choices.

A company's relationship with a host government presents a difficult balancing act. Before we turn to how things go wrong and options for getting it right, we discuss the specific areas of companies' associations with governments that generate criticism from outside stakeholders and trouble managers. We also discuss specific choices and dilemmas that managers face in this arena.

Areas that provoke criticism

There are three specific areas where companies interact with host governments in ways that evoke external criticism and internal angst:

1. Companies provide revenue and other cash transfers to corrupt leaders or governments

Through joint ventures, taxation, sign-up bonuses, bribes, or other fees, companies provide revenue to governments. Corrupt leaders may use such proceeds for personal gain or to support conflict — sometimes against their own people. Especially when this occurs in countries of abject poverty, many people feel that companies have a responsibility to ensure that the revenues they help generate are used for public purposes. Such societal expectations have gained ground through initiatives such as the Extractive Industries Transparency Initiative.

2. Companies inadvertently facilitate human rights abuses by the government

Company infrastructure such as airstrips or roads, or other assets such as vehicles and helicopters, can be misused by authorities. When these are used in conflict, a company may become directly associated with the government's warring position. When this occurs, opposition groups may consider corporate assets to be legitimate military targets. Additionally, international advocacy groups also hold companies accountable for misuse (user-chain abuses) of their assets.

Companies sometimes develop agreements with governments, implicit or explicit, that state security forces will provide security around company operations. If these forces have a poor human rights record, the company will inevitably be negatively associated with these practices. Also, company use of state security forces can provide legitimacy to local commanders who pursue their own conflict agendas.

A third way that a company can face challenges for its support to the human rights violations in a particular country is by adhering to operational conditions imposed by the authorities. These can include government selection of employees, forced population movements, or choice of route of a pipeline. Companies that go along with these conditions are perceived to be supporting an illegitimate government.

Recently, advocacy groups have successfully litigated cases that hold companies accountable for host-government actions. In one case, human rights abuses were alleged to have occurred prior to the arrival of the company during the preparation of the company site. Because the company could have known about the abuse, it was subject to an extensive legal case.

> ❝ Oil and mineral deposits have two particular conditions: governments own them and require licenses for them to be exploited. That means that the extractive industry is directly linked to governments, whether we like it or not. Even if activities are offshore, the reputation of the government directly reflects on companies. Although we work in over 50 countries, the country that poses the biggest risk for us is one is one where our activities entirely take place offshore. ❞
>
> *(Senior vice president of an oil company)*

3. Companies that interact with governments perceived to be oppressive and corrupt are accused of legitimizing them and increasing oppression and corruption

Through their associations and interactions with governments, companies are seen by their critics to be legitimizing oppressive regimes. This is especially true for companies whose presence dates back to colonial times, because they are often seen to be part of the same system. The notion is reinforced when companies are directly linked to oppressive authorities in business: for example, through joint-venture partnerships. Advocacy groups have made the case that the legitimacy provided by the presence of large, Western multinational companies has helped oppressive governments get access to loans from institutions such as the World Bank.

Choices and dilemmas

In response to problematic relationships with governments, corporations have adopted policies and procedures to differentiate themselves from host governments – both out of the need to respect sovereignty and also to try to remain untainted by inappropriate government actions. But they point out that they face several daunting dilemmas as they seek to engage appropriately.

Dilemma 1. Taking a public approach vs. a discreet approach

If a company openly criticizes a government, its approach may be welcomed by advocacy NGOs and the public but it may risk conflict with the government and even expulsion from the country. A behind-the-scenes, discreet approach may be effective in influencing government policies but will not yield public credit for the company. If a company appears to be silent about wrongs, it may be perceived to be supporting the status quo. This can be damning for a corporate reputation when the status quo is seen as oppressive.

> Speaking out risks conflict with the government; remaining silent risks conflict with advocacy groups

Dilemma 2. State-building vs. increasing a government's ability to do harm

A company may work with a government intending to make it more accountable and responsive to its citizens. However, if a company attempts to build government capacity and accountability — for example, by providing workshops or international exchange visits — it may be accused of bolstering the capacity of that government to oppress its people and to fend off international criticism.

One company manager considered providing direct funding to a host government's military to build barracks, noting, "There is nothing more dangerous than a trigger-happy 18-year-old soldier who is homesick standing out in the rain." Others have considered providing funds to ensure adequate pay for soldiers so they would be less likely to prey on local communities. However, critics argue that building military infrastructure or paying soldiers increases the military's power and control over the people.

This dilemma is not limited to countries in a state of crisis. NGOs accuse many companies of taking advantage of weak public capacity to monitor and enforce environmental safeguards. But, when some companies suggest they could provide funds to strengthen the responsible government agencies, the same NGOs accuse the companies of trying to buy favors.

Dilemma 3. Taking responsibility for micro-level issues vs. macro-level governance

Companies argue that their primary responsibility is to ensure improvements for people in the areas of their operations. They feel that they have no leverage or right to exert influence beyond this location. This dilemma is relevant in many places. One striking example is Sudan, where companies working in the south or in the capital are being held accountable for their perceived link (through the provision

Companies feel
they are held to
different standards
in different
countries

of revenues) to the conflict in Darfur, which they feel is out-side their purview.

Further, companies face a dilemma when poor state per-formance in their working environment is not directly related to their corporate presence. For example, in areas of paramilitary or guerrilla activities, an army may abuse local communities. Or a government may fail to make good on promises to pay dismantled militias in areas that are proximate to company sites. In cases like these, managers feel they are powerless to address the problems, but crit-ics insist they should be active in finding solutions at the macro level.

Dilemma 4. Engaging vs. disengaging with governments where there is social or political turmoil

The decision to invest in a country or not, or to stay in or to divest, has both human rights and quality-of-life consequences for local communities and legitimizing political consequences for national governments. It affects local incomes, interna-tional witnessing, the maintenance of international standards that would otherwise not be met, the likelihood of ongoing human rights abuses, and so on. In CEP's

Both staying and
divesting have
consequences for
local communities
from a human
rights perspective

experience, although activists may call for divestment from a country to make an international political point, local communities may disagree and favor growing international investment. The focus of the former is on exerting eco-nomic and political pressure; the focus of the latter is on getting companies to become more active in addressing government policies that affect their immediate quality of life, such as the price of food or the availability of cooking gas, rather than political issues.

Many company representatives argue that divestment is not an option once a company has entered a country because of the negative impacts on local people when a company withdraws. Critics argue that a corporate presence provides both legitimacy and resources to the government that has negative impacts on people's lives.

These four dilemmas highlight the challenges that companies face in trying to bal-ance responding, and being seen to be responding, to outside criticism and trying to make the strongest possible impact on government policies and approaches.

What goes wrong?

Companies want to avoid neo-imperialism. However, in their efforts to abstain from political interference, companies can overshoot in the following ways.

Companies assume that political non-interference means not engaging with governments

Communities and advocacy groups point out that claims of political non-interference are unsatisfactory on three grounds. First, non-interference yields no goodwill or understanding from outsiders. While a company believes that by not speaking out publicly it is taking a neutral position, advocacy groups note that this approach *is* a political statement in favor of the status quo: that is, the regime. Second, a policy of political non-interference is not practical. In reality, companies are always involved in political processes because they sign agreements with and pay taxes to governments. Often they have governmental joint-venture partners. A policy of non-interference provides no guidance on how to conduct such interactions. Third, a non-interference policy can undermine the legitimate business case. Strict adherence to such a policy can backfire when political groups then see corporate assets as legitimate targets for their political and military opposition.

> Pursuing a narrowly defined political non-interference policy creates no outside goodwill, is not practical, and can undermine legitimate business interests

CEP has also seen that political non-interference policies often have a stifling effect on field managers. When interpreting and implementing non-interference, managers tend to feel it is better to be safe than sorry — that is, they feel that they should avoid all contact with government. In extreme cases managers interpret any dealings with government on any issue, other than strictly technical points, as political interference. To be sure they are not interfering, companies end up adopting a policy of non-engagement. Any options for positive engagement are unexplored.

Few companies or joint-venture partners have a deliberate strategy for engagement with authorities

Very few companies or joint-venture partnerships deal with governments in a strategic way. Most companies meet with governments only when there is some issue at stake or when they face technical or operational problems. When they meet, they typically engage only with decision makers in technical departments such as the Ministry of Energy or the Environmental Protection Agency.

Often joint-venture partners do not share information about government contacts or follow the same protocols in meetings with government counterparts. One company arranged for CEP to meet with a senior government official. When CEP arrived at this meeting, we learned that this official had just met with another partner of the same joint venture. The government official concluded that it was obvious the partners did not talk to each other about problematic government policies, so such policies could not really be of much importance to them. He told CEP, "The companies come to me to complain of human rights issues just to satisfy their pressure groups at home, not because they really care."

Options for getting it right

Engagement with government authorities is inevitable. Non-engagement is simply not an option. Therefore the question is not *if* a company should engage with a government but, rather, *how* it should engage!

What does experience show about how corporations can engage with governments without:

- Appearing to be too close to those governments?

- Condoning government policies or actions?

- Risking government sanctions or possible expulsion from the country and loss of access to productive resources or markets?

What is the right course for corporate managers who seek to both respect national sovereignty and live up to, and be seen to be living up to, corporate social responsibility standards?

There is no simple, foolproof formula for getting it right with governments. However, there is a wealth of individualized and context-specific experience that suggests options with positive possibilities for companies.

Initiate discussions before investing

Companies have greater leverage to raise issues and establish constructive operational approaches when they initiate discussions with host countries about possible new investments rather than after they have signed all governmental agreements. In their efforts to attract foreign capital, governments are sometimes willing to hear and make concessions on policies that are important to the company. In this phase, companies can build conditions for investment into their negotiations with a regime. This evidence indicates that companies should therefore resist the tendency to postpone difficult issues. Once a multi-year agreement is signed, this kind of leverage decreases.

Claim and publicize the principles that underlie corporate values

Chapter 10, which covers dealing with advocacy NGOs, notes that critics of corporate complicity with governmental actions do not hope for a corporation to change — or even to try to change — a government. They know that companies cannot, and should not, force their will or perspectives on other people's countries. But they do expect representatives of international corporations to be explicit about their social commitments and corporate codes rather than claiming to be powerless against government and abdicating the responsibility to propagate those values.

In one country where there was nepotism and corruption, civil society groups urged a company to be explicit and public about its operating principles and approaches. When they did so, the company found it yielded two benefits. First, local stakeholders supported the company because people acknowledged that it operated in a respectful, inclusive, and transparent manner. Second, company staff were able to use the statement of principles to explain why they were not able to go along with corrupt practices or violations of human rights.

Conditions for investment during initial negotiations

During negotiations one oil company made the start of operations conditional on peace. It stipulated that it would start operations only when a peace agreement was signed, effective, and sustainable. The exact definitions of effective and sustainable were deliberately left open, and the agreement between the company and the government stated that both parties must agree on the time for starting operations. This gave the company leverage to work with the government to pursue peace that it would not have had if it were locked into a definite starting date.

Another company made its additional investment in a country conditional on commitments from the government to reform its security sector. The company encouraged the government to sign the Voluntary Principles on Human Rights and Security. The company made the point that its investment in the country constituted risk capital. Commitment to the Voluntary Principles would demonstrate the government's commitment to human rights and, thus, reduce the company's risk of being exposed to, and associated with, human rights abuses.

Companies have also negotiated with traditionally secretive governments for the publication of parts of a production-sharing agreement detailing revenue distribution among partners. This has allowed international donors such as the World Bank to demand greater accountability from such governments about how they use their revenue.

Acknowledge that relations and interactions with governments are never politically neutral

Corporations inevitably interact with and have effects on governments, and parts of governments, and vice versa. However, very few companies are willing to recognize openly that they do have inevitable political impacts. To do so is a necessary starting point for engaging responsibly with governments, communities, and advocacy groups about options, dilemmas, and challenges. Denial of this reality is an unhelpful and disingenuous starting point and opens companies to accusations of dishonesty and non-caring about their impacts.

Ask local people what they expect from the company

In the hundreds of interviews that we have conducted through the CEP, only twice did we hear people say that it would be good if the company in question divested from their troubled country. In all other discussions, people told us that they see the presence of a company as a means of achieving a better future. They often indicated that a foreign company has both economic and political positive impacts. In addition, however, communities urge international companies to take a much more active role in advocating on their behalf and to become more, rather than less, politically involved. They want to see the company acting as an ally to them in relations with their government, using its leverage to encourage government to implement good policies. They do not, in general, expect a company to attempt to change official policies at a higher level of political involvement.

Find people in government who will engage positively

No government is monolithic, even those that are adamantly opposed to outside interference. Within every society, we have seen that there are responsible, dedicated civil servants who are genuinely concerned with improving the lives of the citizens. They, too, are frustrated by a lack of sufficient resources and the politicization of decisions. Although a government's stance may be rigidly ideological, individuals within that government vary, and some can always be engaged to achieve common goals.

Companies should focus on the parts of the government that work and find those people within the system who share their objectives in supporting the well-being of citizens. International companies can partner with these individuals and their departments, leverage funds to provide training, and expand possibilities, thereby increasing the space for operation and the legitimacy of these individuals.

Legitimize, support, and expect governments to live up to their own peace and justice commitments

Virtually all governments — even the most repressive — have signed international declarations and/or established departments or focal points on peace, justice, and human rights. These commitments often exist mainly to pacify international demands and the national agencies responsible are deliberately under-funded so they cannot properly execute their mandate. Companies can develop strategies to support such departments financially and reinforce their work. They can set up partnerships with these offices or individuals, support workshops on peace and human rights, and help legitimize the officials responsible for such activities in front of their own colleagues. Companies justify these actions to wary authorities by explaining that they are simply helping the government implement its own policies more effectively.

Develop opportunities for collective corporate action

Evidence shows that when one company tries to address government policies that are problematic, it risks conflict with that government and the policy goes unaddressed. Countries have threatened to expel a company when it made public demands for more revenue transparency. To bolster their position, joint-venture partners and business associations are exploring opportunities for collective action to address government policies that undermine company legitimacy and credibility (for example, as a result of divestment campaigns).

Meet with a broad group of people in government when there is no specific need or agenda

In many countries, it is difficult for a corporate manager to verify how certain decisions are made within the government and how to influence these decisions. Meeting with more people and on more levels (not only at the top) within government, even when there is no immediate issue at stake, can lead to better relations with authorities. Such meetings allow discussion of issues as background rather than points of contention. They allow companies to identify opportunities for engaging on certain issues of common concern with governmental partners. They allow off-the-record raising of issues without expectation of an official governmental response. All of these steps can improve company–government relations in ways that can be used to improve the lives of people in the country.

> ❝ Our company supports a microcredit program and a health program. These programs have provided me with a legitimate excuse to maintain contacts with the Planning Department, and six or seven other ministries, to speak about issues other than oil. And it provides me with a

much better sense of how we can support the government in its own effort to implement good practices. "

(Managing director of a joint-venture partner operating in a country with an oppressive regime)

Create venues for informal interaction

There is nothing like a golf course to allow conversations to build into real relationships. We have seen companies develop annual (or more frequent) golf tournaments where a broad range of company and government officials gather to compete — and interact. Some companies have also successfully created other venues such as workshops or conferences on non-political topics where informal side conversations can lead to personal connections. The purpose of all these interactions is to develop a sufficient level of trust and comfort that a company can exert more influence on issues that improve the lives of people in the countries where they operate.

" As the managing director, I meet with many government officials. Every meeting I have is an opportunity to share the views and principles important to my company, and every meeting is an opportunity for me to discuss some government policies that worry me. "

(Managing director with operations in a country with a non-democratic regime)

Use corporate leverage to lobby for increased government presence

In one country an oil company lobbied an international donor and the host government to establish a Justice Office in a region with high rates of crime and violence. As a result of increased government presence and government follow-up on complaints, people said they felt safer than before. They said that without the lobbying power of the company, this office would not have been established.

Options to mitigate the risk of being associated with human rights abuses

It is important to make a special note of options for working in areas where governments are accused of human rights abuses.

The issue is complex because companies often are forced to associate with the very agencies that commit abuse. Many governments insist that corporations use state security providers to secure their staff and assets. In some countries, authorities feel this is necessary because company activities are vital to the countries' revenues, and they want to protect national assets (such as mineral deposits). In other countries the military is required to generate part of their own budget by providing paid security services to corporate operations.

How can a company get it right in such circumstances?

Insist that the company hire security providers of its own choice

International corporations have created zones of relative peace in the areas surrounding their operations by setting up their own security forces. One company made an arrangement with the army and the police that it would hire people from local communities to guard the gates and provide security on its sites and would provide training and equipment to both their own force and to the army and police. Communities responded positively to this change and reported that their area became much calmer and safer as a result of this agreement. Other companies have made explicit arrangements with state security providers to check the human rights records of commanders assigned to their sites and to be involved in the selection process of security personnel.

Negotiate army behavior in the company's area of operations and the terms of engagement under which the army operates

The Voluntary Principles on Security and Human Rights have provided an incentive, and a tool, for companies to discuss this issue with state security providers. Company agreements with the military can and should include a clause that reaffirms the commitment of the public forces to protect and respect human rights. Some companies explicitly state that they will show no tolerance for human rights violations committed by the military, particularly in their areas of operation. They establish procedures to report and investigate incidents of abuse if they occur. Sometimes they undertake training to ensure that both the company and the security provider have a clear and common understanding about what constitutes acceptable behavior and what does not.

A company–military agreement should include a complaint procedure for communities to report on the army's behavior. The company should ensure that communities know they have a safe venue and procedure for complaints. Some companies have made such mechanisms a part of their community engagement and agreed that, when anyone has a complaint about the army, the company will report this directly to national authorities who have committed to correct any violations.

Rewarding positive performance

In one country, the strategy for providing better living conditions for police and other security providers was to create more sought-after postings. The general manager of one mining company decided to support the military in upgrading the quality of existing barracks and to provide some pool tables, dartboards, and other non-weapon equipment. This gave the general manager leverage to insist on higher levels of training, performance, and behavior of security providers. He was able to insist that poor-performing or misbehaving security providers were transferred away from the area. Since security providers were eager to be posted near the company to live in the improved barracks, he could maintain high levels of professionalism and training among them.

Supporting law and order

When one company found itself in a remote area without a functioning law-and-order mechanism, it subsidized the posting of a prosecutor to the area. At the same time, it engaged in the systematic training of local police forces. The company also set up mechanisms for residents to report incidents of violence to the company, which were then forwarded to the local police. The company argued that, since it would be blamed for poor police behavior, it had a direct interest in ensuring a stable working environment in which the police were seen as fair, constructive, and responsive to demands. This approach reduced crime and violence levels below the national average despite the influx and settlement of thousands of job seekers in the area.

Provide training in international humanitarian law to the military

Where the International Committee of the Red Cross (ICRC) has a presence in a country, it is particularly well positioned to provide international humanitarian law training. ICRC is widely acknowledged as a neutral agency mandated to ensure certain legal protections to civilians and military personnel in conflict areas. Many companies have engaged ICRC to help them improve the standards and performance of local militaries and policy forces. Alternatively, some companies have paid for army officials to attend international human rights courses where they have been able to meet military officials from other countries and exchange experiences.

Other approaches taken by companies with regard to human rights

- Mandatory human rights training for (contractor) staff
- Open invitation to international human rights groups to audit corporate human rights policies and practices
- Discussions with national staff about human rights in the specific context. This generates options to ensure the company's compliance with international standards.

Options for revenue transparency

As the concept of user-chain responsibility gains public support, companies are increasingly being held accountable for how the revenues they generate are used. Clearly a company cannot tell a government how it can spend its money. There are, however, options ensuring that funds are used for public welfare, rather than private gain or warfare, which focus on helping local groups hold their leadership accountable.

Local groups need four things in order to effectively hold their government accountable, and companies can help them in a variety of ways.

1. Access to information about revenue flows

Ensure public access to revenue figures. Companies that sign up to the Extractive Industries Transparency Initiative make their revenues public on a periodic basis. They routinely publish the amount of revenues paid to a government in their annual reports and/or in local newspapers. Other companies can follow this precedent. Where companies want to ensure that revenues are used in their areas of operation, some have negotiated tax credit funds with the national treasury. Through such an agreement, some portion of company taxes is allocated to local development such as school maintenance, upgrade of infrastructure, or other projects that fit within the government's regional plan.

2. Organizational skills and capacity to use information effectively

Support civil society groups in developing capacity to engage government personnel. Some companies invite NGOs to provide workshops or training to local communities. Others provide such training themselves or provide venues where government and citizens can meet on neutral ground.

3. A safe venue for civil society groups to come together for discussion and planning

Use corporate convening power and the safe environment of the company premises to invite civil society groups that otherwise cannot meet to discuss sensitive issues such as state corruption or state violence. In countries where the security situation is fragile, civil society groups may not be comfortable organizing a meeting to discuss government accountability and responsiveness. A company can arrange meetings for such discussions, ensuring that the official topic of the gathering is not politically controversial.

4. Capacity of local authorities to constructively respond to community requests

Work with, and increase capacity of, local authorities. Companies should also provide training for local authorities to help them become responsive to community approaches. Some companies arrange workshops where both civil society groups and local officials can meet together. The relationships established during these trainings, and officials' increasing comfort with assertive communities, can lead to more responsive local governance. Other companies work together with international institutions and donors to offer good governance training to local officials.

Summary

Communities want and expect to receive government services. In reality, many feel these expectations are not met. They hope a company's presence will generate more government interest in their region. Therefore, a company's relationships with state authorities cannot be seen as separate from their relationships with local communities. We have seen evidence that companies' efforts to engage constructively with governments have had a positive effect on the quality of life of local communities and yielded positive perceptions of the company in the community.

Indicators of positive government relations

- The government is providing public services in the area of company operations rather than expecting the company to do so. If the government has limited capacities, the company is working with existing capacities and supporting them to address public service needs.

- The government is (increasingly) responsive to community members on issues of public safety and security.

- Company policy and practice enable the government to avoid corruption and allegations of corruption.

- Company and government together are transparent about payments and other interactions so that communities can hold them accountable.

SECTION III

13

Internal management issues that determine the success or failure of external relations

Many managers do not see any relationship between their company's internal organization and the issues of community relations. Some feel that management issues are internal matters that fall outside the scope of a community-related assessment. However, analysis of evidence gathered by CEP has shown that the manner in which the internal departments of a company are structured and relate to each other has a direct impact on the success of a company's relations with its community stakeholders.

How internal organizational issues impact external relations

The principle message of this book is that the way a company conducts its day-to-day core activities is more important than its community relations programs in determining how the company is perceived by local stakeholders. Although external or community relations departments are the primary communicators with local people and are expected to be responsible for maintaining cordial community relations, it is the behaviors, policies, and practices of *other* departments that affect people's perceptions of the company and determine how they behave toward the company.

Decisions that matter most to local people are made by departments other than those designated to be in charge of community relations. The Human Resources Department determines who gets hired and how. The Contracting Department sets policies that can favor local contractors and suppliers or make it difficult for local businesses to benefit from the corporate presence. The Accounting Department can facilitate administrative procedures and ensure speedy payments of compensation or set complicated and delaying administrative requirements. Guards at the company gate, managed by the Security Department, are the first point of contact with the company and thus affect a community's perceptions of the company. Whether company security policies communicate mistrust (armed guards, dogs, fences) or trust of and openness to communities affects attitudes and behaviors. The policies and practices of the Seismic teams (even when operating offshore), the Drilling Department, the Operations Department, the Construction team, and the Health, Safety, and Environment team are all *indirectly* related to company–community issues but have a *direct* impact on how the company is perceived. Even when staff from these departments do not directly engage with communities, the way they drive, control dust, or deal with culturally sensitive areas can all undermine, or support, company–community relations. All the best efforts of an External Affairs Department can have little impact if the hiring procedures of a company are seen as unfair, security policies are seen to be oppressive, or local contractors are not paid on time.

Table 13.1 provides some examples that show how different departments have impacts on company–community relations.

The example of safety

In virtually every industrial company, safety issues feature prominently. Staff are reminded in multiple ways about the importance of this issue. The first thing one sees on arriving at a company is a billboard displaying the number of consecutive days that have passed without an accident. From administrative assistants to engineers, everybody in the organization knows the importance of safety, owns the issue, and understands that his or her actions can have an impact on the company's safety record, either negatively or positively.

Because it is understood that a company's safety performance is affected by all company staff, safety departments are typically small and play primarily a support, monitoring, and coordinating role. The implementation of safety policies takes place on all levels in the organization, and all employees are held accountable for

Table 13.1 **Impacts on company–community relations**

Department	Negative impacts	Positive impacts
Human resources	Local people perceive that only outsiders are hired	Hiring more local people; respectful retrenchment of staff
Security	Security personnel at the gate are disrespectful to communities	Engagement to increase law and order in the wider mine area
Projects	Violation of sacred sites; entering land without the owners' permission	Dust control efforts; fair and adequate compensation for crops and land
Accounting	Payment to local contractors is delayed	Helping local stakeholders overcome administrative obstacles
Contracts	Selection is based on criteria that local contractors will not be able to meet	Adding behavioral guidelines for contractors as annex to the contract
Health, safety, and environment	Spills are not cleaned up	Safe driving speeds, community health efforts, environmental responsibility

their behavior with regard to safety. Because of this, there is no need for a large safety department.

The organization of the safety department differs from the specialized departments such as surveying, contracting, or human resources. Ownership and accountability for these departments' activities rest primarily within the departments themselves. It is assumed that only specialists can, or should, perform these activities and that they should have control over the outcomes of their activities.

The functions of external relations departments are similar to those of safety departments. Both safety and community-related issues are affected by the behavior of all staff and directly contribute to the ability of a company to reach its goals. Achieving good community relations requires that an external relations department take a coordinating and monitoring role and engage all other company departments in analyzing and owning the processes by which their actions affect community perceptions.

In reality, most external relations departments are structured (and function) as specialized departments. When any company operation creates tension with communities, handling this constructively is considered to be too difficult for the department that created the problem. Hence, community relations "experts" are brought in to solve the problem. Very few departments have their own community relations coordinator (as they might have a safety coordinator) who is held accountable for tensions between the company and community caused by his or her department.

As a result, and in contrast to the safety department, the external relations department ends up playing an implementing rather than a coordinating role. In practice, community relations staff are held responsible for outcomes over which they have little control simply because of the way a company is organized (see Fig. 13.1).

Figure 13.1 **Accountability vs. control**

Department	Level of accountability	Level of control
Survey Accounting Projects	Department held accountable for outcome and implementation of projects ⬆	Department has a great degree of control over the outcomes of their projects ⬆
Safety	Department plays a monitoring and coordinating role, each staff member held accountable for his or her own behavior ⬇	Department has a low degree of control over level of safety. Individual staff members control level of overall safety ⬇
External relations	Department held accountable for creating a positive relationship with local communities ⬆	Department has a low degree of control over the behavior of other departments. These control overall relations ⬇

When an external relations department is the sole location for community relations experts, this often means that their expertise is required to resolve community problems only after they have already occurred. The external relations department acts as a *de facto* fire-fighting brigade, and the company operates in a continuing crisis-response mode with regard to community issues.

The corporate perspective on external relations: add-on activity or key success factor?

In its site visits, CEP has been tracing the question of how management sees the role of external relations. Do managers consider external relations to be an add-on to core activities or do they see this role as key to the overall success of the company? Unfortunately, we have found that most managers consider community relations to be an afterthought that is given attention either because investors require it or because serious disruptive problems have arisen. Core activities of the corporation are perceived as the determinants of company success. Because technical operations make money for the company and external relations cost money, managers see community relations as an add-on. This mind-set has implications:

1. External relations activities are not held to the same standards that are applied to operational activities.

2. Internal management systems and procedures become obstacles to effective community engagement.

3. The department in charge of community relations is not given the right resources (staff, budget) at the right time to perform effectively.

As a result, the department charged with community relations can be set up for failure (see Fig. 13.2); it can meet neither the expectations of the broader organization nor those of local communities.

Figure 13.2 **External relations: cycle of ineffectiveness**

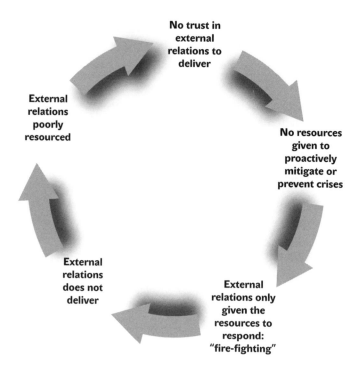

1. External relations activities are not held to the same standards applied to operational activities

When a company considers community relations to be an add-on to corporate operations, it very often holds these activities to lower standards and bases them on an inferior analysis that other departments in the company would never get away with.

Poor definition of what stakeholder engagement aims to achieve

Companies are remarkably non-strategic in linking their community relations activities with the objectives they aim to achieve. Many lack a clear and measurable definition of what constitutes successful community relations. Managers describe the purpose of community projects vaguely as "creating goodwill," "maintaining a license to operate," or "establishing a legacy." Short-term success is narrowly defined as avoiding negatives such as demonstrations, roadblocks, or other disruptions. Long-term success is rarely well defined.

Without clear objectives and lacking a strategy that links activities to objectives, a company cannot develop a systematic approach for achieving — or measuring — success. Most have no way to determine if they are on the path toward achieving their (implicit!) objectives.

Poor problem analysis

With technical processes, corporate managers — especially those trained as engineers — have clear input, flow-through, and output expectations. Unexpected outcomes are seen as a challenge to be analyzed and corrected.

When community engagement efforts result in unexpected negative outcomes, the reaction is often quite different. Rather than seeing these as a problem to be solved, managers typically react by claiming powerlessness. We have heard them say, "There is nothing we can do. Communities' behavior is totally unpredictable, and you never know what to expect." Such reactions are counterproductive; they do not lead a company to do serious problem analysis or to develop options for addressing problems.

It is not difficult to find out why community relations problems arise. People are usually candid and straightforward in explaining how they see the issues and what it is that bothers them. A flow-through analysis works with communities as it does with a pipe — when there is an unexpected outcome, it is possible to trace various aspects of operations and to find what needs to be fixed (re-engineered). The point is that few companies systematically do this kind of problem analysis in relation to community issues.

Staff performance indicators measure the wrong thing

Community relations performance indicators are often based on inputs and outputs, rather than on outcomes and impacts. Companies mistakenly measure community relations programs by how many schools they build or how many public meetings they organize. These are inputs. Or they may count how many students attend school or how many community people attended a meeting. These are outputs. Neither inputs nor outputs provide information about what happened as a result of company efforts. Did students learn something in the school that is useful? Did they go on to higher education or get a job? Did people leave the community meeting feeling as if they had a real stake in their futures with the company? Did the meeting address issues in problem-solving ways?

The *numbers* of schools or meetings or other inputs do not say anything about their *quality* and their effects on people's lives. It is important to develop methods of assessment that are attentive to whether things are getting better for people, or worse, or whether the quality of their lives is improving or deteriorating as a result of company actions.

We will discuss the measuring of success in more detail in the next chapter.

Measuring success . . . or failure?

A company organized a public meeting, inviting dignitaries from various communities to the company premises. After one hour several chiefs left the meeting accusing the company representative of being arrogant and of not listening to community complaints. "We were here to give them a chance, but I'm going to tell my [armed] boys in the bush to teach the company a lesson," one chief said.

The company representative later said that the meeting had been a success. It was mentioned in the annual report as an indicator of company involvement with community leaders.

Community relations activities are budget-driven rather than achievement-driven

The budgets of most company departments are based on what is needed to do the job effectively. However, the driving question for external relations often is not, "How much is needed to achieve our specific impact objectives?" but "How much do we need to be seen to be spending to convince communities that we care about them?" Furthermore, when an external relations department is under pressure to spend its budget within a fiscal year, getting the money out can become more important than meeting some real objective. Communities complain that in such situations soft skills training and other low-cost programs are sidelined in favor of more expensive infrastructure projects that are not based on a genuine assessment of the relative need for and impacts of the projects. Many companies intend to stay in a location for decades, so they want to establish a long-term relationship with key groups. However, they allocate their community budgets in ways that are unrelated to their objective of establishing and maintaining a long-term relationship. This is simply inefficient.

Budgeting community relations this way furthers cynicism and irritation in communities who perceive that the company prioritizes public relations over a genuine concern for local community growth and progress.

2. Internal management systems and procedures are obstacles to effective stakeholder engagement

When community relations are seen as an add-on to a company's technical activities rather than as a core activity, management systems to achieve effective community relations are weak. Management systems often represent obstacles to positive community relations. Obstacles have to do with lack of timely information, a lack of standardization, internal reward systems that favor production targets over community relations, and the like.

External relations follow core processes rather than informing them

A major obstacle to the effectiveness of any external relations department is its lack of involvement in the project design. Technical departments often assume there is no need to involve external relations staff in early phases of a project. The working assumption is that community relations people are there simply to facilitate the technical processes and make things work after the project is designed and technical decisions are made. However, once decisions are made, it is difficult to inject a community perspective.

A disconnect between the "soft" and the technical departments is unfortunate in two ways. First, when external relations staff are included in project design, they may be able to identify opportunities for expedited implementation that the technical people may not see. Second, if external relations people are not involved in project design, community problems may arise that could have been prevented (e.g., building on a disputed area or sacred ground).

When external relations departments are under pressure to satisfy requirements from technical departments that do not consult them until there is a problem, they become only a negotiation wing of operations rather than a system for opening avenues to obtain local support and goodwill. Negotiations, compensation payments, and discussion of agreements may consume so much of the external relations staff's time that they cannot relate to local people on any other basis. In such cases, companies become legitimate targets for community demands rather than partners in achieving common goals.

Lack of standardization

Whereas most companies have protocols, SOPs or other tools to standardize technical or safety requirements, external relations standardization is generally limited to a one-page community relations statement.

Many companies leave important community-relations decisions to individual judgment rather than basing them on strategic policies. While this may provide an opportunity for dedicated staff to respond swiftly and appropriately to a given local situation, if individual decision-making power is not accompanied by regularized checks and balances (as can be the case with companies that have no clear standards or a planned strategy to achieve agreed goals), the organization is vulnerable to charges of favoritism or other questionable practices. One senior manager, commenting on how some community relations staff work to get kickbacks from local contractors, observed,

> " The employees who want to do bad stuff find it is best to keep a sense of chaos. This lets them work with contractors they favor rather than putting contracts out for bid, using the excuse that a job needs to be done quickly and that only certain contractors can be trusted. "

The problems created by this lack of standardization are compounded when multiple departments are dealing with the same stakeholders without a coordinated approach. Especially during the construction of major projects, communities may deal with several liaison officers including the projects community officer, the operations community officer, and the contractor community officer. Each may have a different approach, budget, and objective. If, for example, salary levels for non-skilled labor are not synchronized across departments, differences can lead to community protests.

It matters who owns the budget for community projects. Different departments have different interests. In some companies, over half of the community budget is allocated to units that have short-term tasks such as completing a construction phase. The approach taken by units with short-term objectives differs markedly from the approaches of departments that want a long-term relationship with local communities. For example, the goal of a construction crew is to finish a project within budget and on time. Community demands are assessed using a short-term cost–benefit analysis with production targets as the primary objective. Not included in short-term calculations are relationships, reputation, long-term consequences, or other community variables.

Communities are often aware of these — sometimes conflicting — objectives within a company. When they know that the company needs to meet short-term targets, they may adopt delaying techniques (some say, "Time is on our side, not theirs") to increase community benefits. It is tempting for the company's project managers to promise projects to "buy the peace" for the duration of their engagement. This can lead to high expectations and unfulfilled promises that the operations department (which will be on site for many years and often has relatively lower budgets) will have to deal with. The Ijaw group in Nigeria has an expression in their language called the "kpeke strategy" (*kpeke* means shaking). They explain that, "If you shake companies enough, you will get anything out of them." Sharp increases in the external relations budgets of oil companies in the Niger Delta from 1990 to the present show this strategy has been successful for community people whose only interest is in extracting direct and immediate benefits from companies.

Reward structures

In most companies, reward structures are designed to increase production rather than to steer behavior (safety awards being the exception). If companies structure financial rewards, such as bonuses, largely (or solely) to promote success in reaching quarterly production targets, this can undermine constructive community engagement approaches. CEP has seen that sometimes when criminal groups disrupt oil operations by hijacking a rig or occupying a flow station, company managers calculate the financial costs of meeting the criminals' demands relative to the costs of lost production and, on this calculation, give in to the demands. This, of course, rewards criminal behavior and, possibly and unintentionally, finances purchases of new weapons to be used for a future hijacking.

> ⁶⁶ These boys occupied a flow station and demanded that we build a hospital for the community. Of course I refused, as I did not want to be blackmailed or to negotiate under pressure. They already told me how many barrels per day I was losing and even calculated the daily cost to the company. I called my boss to explain the situation. He asked me if I was crazy and ordered me to promise the hospital as it would be much cheaper to pay for it than to stop production for several days. I know these guys will be back when their money runs out. It will be sooner than we will be able to build that hospital. ⁹⁹
>
> *(Project manager of an oil operation)*

A heavy focus on reaching short-term production targets (ounces, barrels, acreage acquisitions, or a specific number of community signatures) can put pressure on staff to make short-term choices that can have long-term negative consequences.

Short-term production targets trigger chain reactions:

- Pressure to purchase land can force a company to buy land from illegitimate owners and lead to subsequent double land payments.

- Pressure to purchase land quickly can lead to inflated prices. Communities know that if they resist long enough the price that a company is willing to pay will rise. This continually creates new precedents.

- Under pressure to deliver a community representative, external relations staff may choose the wrong representative when the leadership structure in a community is not clear.

- If external relations staff are under pressure to get a signed commitment from communities, they may make promises they know they cannot fulfill or pay signatories to the agreement just to meet the target.

- If in the face of work interruptions due to community unrest, staff relies on security to resume work before the causes of the community unrest are addressed, this may deepen community suspicion that the company does not care about it and provide an incentive for the community to provoke an even bigger interruption in order to be heard.

A short-term approach may also mean that problems are postponed rather than addressed. When a company behaves in a way that leads communities to conclude that it will soon leave, local people's demands for immediate benefits rise. When this occurs, companies may support projects that fit within a short time-frame (because people have demanded these) but ignore longer-term activities that could have provided more lasting benefits for communities' well-being. If communities knew that a company intended to stay involved over a long time, they could also plan more wisely and focus on longer-term investments rather than short-term gains.

Who's paying the ransom?

The assignment of different expenses to different budgets can result in inadvertent negative community relations that are costly to a company. In one area, international company staff was kidnapped and ransom paid. These payments came from a budget line maintained in the company's headquarters in Europe. On the other hand, the country manager received his rewards for pursuing high production levels and incurring low local costs. A closer look revealed that he was deeply criticized by local-hire staff for underpaying them while pushing their productivity. They, therefore, had found that they could increase their incomes by informing community-level criminal groups of the movements of international staff and where and when they could most easily be kidnapped. When ransom was paid, these local staff received a cut of the payment. If the in-country manager had to pay the high ransoms from his budget or if these events had been included in his annual performance bonus, the manager would likely have made different decisions.

3. External relations programs are not given the right resources at the right time to perform effectively

The third consequence of considering community issues as an add-on to the corporate core activities is that the responsible departments are not given the right resources, at the right time, to do their jobs effectively.

Budget procedures mean resources are not available when most needed

Over the chapters of this book we have consistently made the point that positive company–community relations cannot be bought. We have stressed the importance of *how* over *what*, of transparency, engagement, fairness, and respect. We have consistently noted that building a positive relation with local communities is *not* all about money!

When they get this message, managers may assume that this means the company should do nothing at all that involves direct community relations programming. This is not the case.

A company *should* invest — seriously and early — in developing its capacity for ongoing community consultation and engagement; it should establish a permanent and effective grievance office; it should develop and discuss with communities an influx management plan. These investments require resources for salaries, training, offices, logistics, and so on. Especially in the (pre)construction phase, such investment should be directed toward staff competences and internal systems more than on community projects. These investments need to be made, and maintained, for effective community relations.

Many external affairs directors are frustrated by the fact that, in times of cost cutting, their budgets are the first to be reviewed. When relations with communities are going well and there have been no recent production disruptions, managers often ask community relations departments to take a budget cut. The expectation is that they can achieve their results with fewer resources. When there are community-based crises and conflicts, managers are motivated to spend more (and, as noted above, inadvertently reward violence rather than supporting more reasonable and peaceful community members). One senior manager told us that he recognized these perverse incentives. He noted, "It is in the interest of our security and community relations staff to report daily on the tensions and conflicts they see. If they report that all is calm, we will surely cut their budgets and reduce their staff." Evidence shows that the costs of reacting to conflict are many times higher than the costs of conflict prevention (consider, for example, the costs associated with a loss of production for only one day!). However, many of the budgeting and other reward systems in companies reinforce tendencies to feed conflict and undermine prevention strategies.

> ** The Projects Department has no clue how hard we are working to make sure there is no work stoppage due to community unrest. When there are no problems, they think that we are simply lazy. To us, a demonstration is a bad sign that we would like to prevent. But it is only when we have a demonstration that they recognize our role and feel that we are useful. Do we really need a negative event to take place before we are recognized? **
>
> *(Community liaison officer of a mining company)*

A second reason that community relations budgets may come under early scrutiny is the lack of international guidelines and legal requirements for working with communities. One need only compare this with requirements for environmental management to understand this point. International and national legal requirements stipulate specific environmental studies that must be conducted before projects are started; they specify control mechanisms and mitigation measures that must be put in place before licenses are issued or investment funds provided. Because these are formal, legal requirements, the costs are considered capital expenditures and are undisputed. In community relations, where there are no legislative stipulations, it is up to the discretion of a company to determine how much to spend. Community relations budgets are optional.

Many companies calculate the budget available for community relations as a percentage of their operations expenditures. When production expands and the operational budget increases, the external relations department's budgets increase as well. When production decreases, the budgets available for community issues also fall.

However, the need for community-related activities and the resources to fund them does not follow the production schedule. During the pre-construction phase, a company must not only develop its own internal capacity to address community relations, it must also deal with community expectations, organize community consultations at multiple levels, acquire land, build infrastructure, and prepare communities for the upcoming project phases. These things cost money. During construction, the need for public engagement may decrease as people get jobs, see their economy become more vibrant due to compensation money, salaries, and contracts, and enjoy new services that are available as a result of the corporation's presence.

The need for external relations resources increases again toward the end of the construction phase when unskilled employment opportunities wane and local communities have come to expect continuing improvements in their lives. Working with communities to address this transition can require more meetings, community visits, and efforts to develop employment options for people who lose their jobs. Once operations have begun, it is again possible that new resource allocations for community involvement become unnecessary if a company has developed a trusting working relationship with people. But again toward the end of a project, it may be important for a company to increase its financial commitments to help communities prepare for its departure. Not recognizing this, companies usually decrease resource allocations to community relations as production decreases. It would be far wiser for managers to assign funds to external relations efforts in relation to the concerns that are on people's minds and the issues they are dealing with rather than in relation to levels of spending on company operations.

Figure 13.3 provides a visual representation of how the resources needed to fund external relations activities during the various phases of the project cycle do not match the resources that are typically made available by companies during these phases. Although this graph is representational only, it signals that, especially in the feasibility phase and towards closure, community relations efforts are generally under-funded, whereas during operations resources are often available but comparatively less needed.

Figure 13.3 **External affairs resources needed vs. resources budgeted**

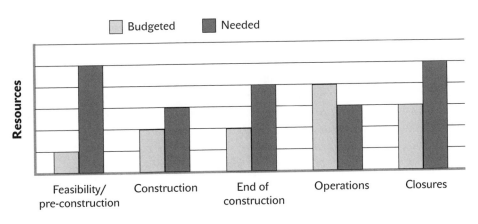

Inattention to staff skills and support

When companies do not consider external relations to be an essential core competency for effective operations, the status of people assigned to external relations departments will be relatively low. Sometimes this means that little thought is given to the specific expertise needed to be effective in this area. The evidence from field experience is that effective community relations efforts can be staffed either by people trained and experienced in community-level work or by line engineers who have experience in other company departments. The skill advantage of people with community experience is clear. They are comfortable in community settings, they have a framework for understanding community dynamics, and often they are recruited because of specific language and cultural skills that support their immediate engagement with local people.

Alternatively, when an engineer with full knowledge of the technical side of operations also takes on community relations, there are other advantages. First, people who have worked in technical departments have collegial networks which may help them work with these departments to integrate community relations concerns into the company's daily operations (as described above in relation to safety protocols). Second, people who understand the technical aspects of company work may also be well placed to anticipate operational issues that affect communities and to plan ahead for these, rather than reacting to them when they come up unexpectedly. Also, engineers respect engineers as tough thinkers and this may mean that they respect and treat seriously the ideas that come out of the community relations departments more than when they think the department is staffed with "soft" thinkers who "waste time in the communities just chatting with people."

In both cases, however, CEP has observed that most staff on the front lines of community engagement are not experienced or trained in how to handle difficult — even dangerous — situations. They are expected to chair public meetings, handle anger and threats, negotiate win-win solutions to problems and, in general, serve as conflict resolution experts without the specific skill set that such tasks require. Whether they hire community experts or engineers to do their community relations work, managers and human resources departments need to be as serious about the skill set needed by these staff as they are about the skill sets required by operational departments.

Further, staff who are responsible for ensuring positive community relations need other kinds of company support as much as operational departments need these. We have often seen external relations staff who do not have regular access to sufficient vehicles (to visit communities) or to external expertise when it is needed. It is clearly difficult to develop a strategic approach to community partnership if one must hitch a ride with operational staff whenever they happen to be going in the direction of the community one wants to visit!

In addition, few companies have an ongoing and systematic context-analysis approach linked to community relations. Community incidents are not systematically investigated, documented, verified, and analyzed; they are typically written up on incident report cards and filed. This is in stark contrast to the normal investigative procedure that is triggered in cases of safety incidents even though a community crisis may have the same impact on a company (e.g., a one-day work interruption). In safety cases, companies fly in experts to review procedures and a case is not closed until the company has done everything possible to prevent the reoccurrence of the incident. There is no such response when work interruptions are caused by community issues. Were management systems in place to ensure a serious, expert-led review in the event of community disruptions, the knowledge base on which strategic community interactions would be based would be greatly improved. One could expect significant reductions in community incidents.

Same cost, different responses

One company faced a strike of workers from local communities over employment conditions. The processing plant went down for one day (costing hundreds of thousands of dollars) and the company suffered a blow to its image which was widely exposed in the local media. Company managers acknowledged that, if a safety incident had caused the same damage to the company, an analysis would have been conducted to determine the cause and an action plan with monitoring requirements written to prevent repetition of the incident. Instead, two months after the fact, the basic causes of the strike had still not been addressed and these began to affect broader company–community relations.

The consequences of add-on external relations

The same problems keep coming back

One important indicator that an external relations department is reactive rather than proactive is the recurrence of the same problems again and again. This may happen when company staff from departments other than the external relations, who are not held accountable for their impacts on communities, do things that cause problems. When community relations staff are expected to correct crises caused by other company departments, they repeatedly address the symptoms of the problems but not the behaviors or policies that caused them. No institutional learning takes place and the same mistakes are made over and over again.

Community relations departments grow into kingdoms

The formal and informal reward systems of most corporations emphasize size. Prestige and standing are linked to big budgets or big departments. Large departments are more important than small departments.

In this culture, it is not surprising that, when external relations is isolated as a separate departmental responsibility rather than integrated into all operations, the staff responsible for company–community relations also want to grow their department. We noted above that sometimes external relations (and security) departments emphasize problems over solutions in order to prove that they are needed. The more problems a company faces with communities, the larger the external relations budget, the more people who are hired to deal with the problems, the more responsibilities these staff are given, the higher the status of the department in the company, and the higher their rewards. A corporate culture that rewards bigness indirectly provides a disincentive for effective community relations.

Big departments rewarded for large responsibilities reinforce the tendency of such departments not to share responsibility. If safety departments provide a better model for the design of external relations departments, then sharing responsibility with all operational staff is critical. Further, for healthy involvement of communities, staff responsible for this involvement need to find ways to reduce their roles and increase the efficacy and responsibility of community-based organizations, local NGOs, and local governments. When company reward systems encourage isolation, some external relations departments have become among the most resistant to partnering. This runs counter to all effective community relations work.

Unethical business practices and corruption

Corruption in community relations departments is not often discussed. There is evidence, however, that the combination of a lack of clarity about community relations objectives, under-trained and under-appreciated community relations staff, and a budget-driven approach can contribute to misuse of funds by external relations staff.

There are three reasons for discussing business practices and corruption in this section. First, many loyal company staff describe the profoundly demoralizing effect that company corruption can have on their own activities. Second, when community people see that a company does not aggressively combat corruption within the organization, whether it is in the external relations or any other department, they conclude that it is acceptable to use any means to profit from the company's presence. If a company does not hold its own employees accountable, then why should community people behave more honorably? Third, when community relations staff misappropriate funds intended for community projects, even the staff who are themselves involved in these unethical practices conclude that the company is not serious about its relationships with local communities. Over time it becomes acceptable for staff to deceive the company and profit from diversion of community funds, and it is hard to find whistle-blowers as the practice becomes common and no one is held accountable.

In CEP's experience, it seems that projects that have the poorest company–community relations are also the ones with the highest levels of corruption by company staff. When corruption is tolerated, it spreads in many directions. In some countries, retired employees provide information to criminal gangs about the company's vulnerabilities – information for which they are well paid. In one country, a civil society team hired by the company to monitor its community projects expected to visit a multi-million-dollar hospital that the company had financed. They reviewed the report of an external accountant who had approved all the expenditures for this hospital. However, on the site where the hospital was supposed to be, the team found a soccer field! One would conclude that a number of people, many officially linked to the company, had to have been involved in such a large scam. It is not surprising that this kind of diversion has a direct and important impact on a company's attempts to establish healthy relations with local communities.

Options for getting it right

Companies have used a number of different approaches to ensure that their internal structure is aligned with and supports their intent to establish and maintain constructive community relations.

Transform external relations from firefighter to internal service provider

Some external relations managers have found ways to demonstrate that their department can be most effective when they are included in the decision-making processes in all phases of the project.

Making this change is entirely within the control of community relations departments and is generally well received by other departments. Some examples follow:

- Community relations managers have organized meetings to explain the types of services they can provide to each department, using phrases such as "internal clients" and "offering uninterrupted access to land" and other language that convinces company departments that community relations staff are genuinely interested in supporting the revenue-generating departments.

- One department negotiated a service-level agreement with the various "clients" (other company staff and departments) within the organization. This agreement specified the conditions that needed to be met to ensure delivery of community relations expectations. They successfully used the agreement to ensure that they were involved in all operational decisions that affected communities and were informed in time to allow community engagement in decisions where appropriate. Having regular and early discussions with various departments about their plans (e.g., specific dates a department needed to be able to access a community) made it possible for the community relations staff to develop a strategy for fulfilling their commitments in the given time-frame. This kind of involvement of community relations staff in overall planning supports respectful and transparent interaction with community people.

- Some companies have enacted a policy that all new projects need internal approval by the external relations department before they can be implemented in order to ensure that local stakeholders are consulted and that they agree to plans.

Broaden the ownership for external relations within the organization

To broaden ownership for community issues and involvement on the part of the responsible technical departments, some external relations departments have:

- **Developed an induction module** on community affairs for every new staff member. Such modules raise awareness about how every employee affects community relations, sets out some *dos* and *don'ts* for staff and company behavior and explain the types of services external relations staff can provide to support other departments.

- **Trained security officers** to ensure that the company's approach to security is based on approaching communities as partners, rather than as risks, to the company.

- **Invited other staff to join them in community meetings and presentations.** To demystify community engagement, external relations staff invite their colleagues from the technical departments to join them in community visits or public meetings where they explain and discuss upcoming company activities to communities and government officials.

- **Produced a short weekly local context update** that informs staff in all departments about rumors, incidents, community issues, etc., to raise awareness of and appreciation for community ideas, sensibilities, and priorities.

- **Reviewed policies through a community lens.** Some external relations departments have offered to review the policies and plans of other departments to identify "low-hanging fruit" ideas for how operational activities can improve company–community relations. This has led to refreshing and creative ideas. For example, a geology department developed wireless technologies to limit damage to people's crops that would have occurred with land lines, a project department taught local entrepreneurs to write a business plan, and a construction department used the soil from company excavations to level community soccer fields.

- **Integrated community issues in company staff career paths.** To signal the importance of community relations in achieving company goals, a company can ensure that all up and coming company leaders are assigned a job in an external relations department sometime in their career. This approach builds a company leadership that understands the centrality and complexity of community issues and buttresses the prestige and credibility of external relations departments.

- **Integrated attention to community issues into reward structures.** Increasingly, companies are incorporating the quality of the relationship with local stakeholders in their performance reviews for all staff. Some include the number of community incidents as one factor determining bonuses or provide company-wide awards for staff of departments that are judged to have made a positive contribution to company–community relations.

Ensure the external relations budget is realistic

We know which systems and protocols are important in establishing a constructive and effective community engagement program. Such basics include a local content policy, a community-monitoring mechanism, regular (quarterly) public meetings in communities, an effective grievance procedure, etc. As companies determine how much to spend on community relations, they can calculate the costs associated with setting up these kinds of systems or protocols compared to the costs of community crises (costs of down days, for example, or contractor claims due to community unrest) that may occur if such systems are not in place.

Front-load activities

Companies that have "front-loaded" money and staff to establish cordial relations with local communities as they arrive on site repeatedly describe such early expenditures as good investments and wise business decisions. They point out that the company–community relationships established in the feasibility phase of a project enabled them to clarify mutual roles and responsibilities that formed the basis for solving subsequent problems. Dealing with high community and government expectations early in a project requires resources and staff time.

Ensure standardization and coordination in external relations

In order to ensure that all company departments and contractors operate with similar standards, companies have:

- **Standardized salary levels and benefits for similar jobs in all departments and for contractors**

- **Used contracts to enforce standardization.** Some have attached a code of behavior for community approaches as an annex to employees' contracts. Failure to comply with these annexes is considered a breach of contract.

- **Set up central hiring systems (also for contractors).** Some companies hire all non-skilled labor for all contractors to ensure maximum job opportunities for local people and to avoid divisions between groups over hiring policies.

- **Named a single focal point for the community–company relations.** Some companies name one point or person for community-related matters for all departments and all contractors to avoid communities playing different departments off against each other.

Build a community relations team

One mine organized a one-week team-building exercise for their construction and their operating crews. As a result, the construction crew became more receptive to the advice and suggestions of the operating crew whose job it was to take over after construction was complete. Because the operating crew was committed to establishing long-term positive community relations, the way that the construction crew behaved was very important in establishing the early company–community relationship. The construction phase was finalized on budget and on time and with support of the local community.

Increase in-house capacity to address conflict

Some companies are beginning to arrange training for their staff in conflict resolution so that they are more comfortable dealing with community pressures and have appropriate skills for doing so. Some use local conflict experts whom they can also bring in for support if they are needed.

Some also establish standard procedures for dealing with conflicts, such as policies to make no cash payments under threat or to hire no ghost workers to undermine community demands for jobs. Some systematically analyze the causes of all incidents that cross certain thresholds, such as a work interruption that lasts longer than a designated period of time.

Figure 13.4 **Questions to determine whether your corporate structure creates a positive approach to external stakeholder relations**
(continued over)

THE QUESTION	WHAT THE ANSWER TELLS US
To whom does the External Relations Department (ERD) report? If not to the Managing Director, who are the managers in between? What background do they have (legal? PR?)	How important ERD is within the organization. Degree of recognition of the role and purpose of the department
Who controls the budget of the ERD? If more than one department is in control, what are their interests and approaches?	Provides a sense of the position of the ERD relative to other departments and identifies if approaches are compatible, effective, and implemented to further long-term cordial relations
Does the company have a system in place whereby communities can communicate problems in a non-violent manner (such as a grievance procedure)?	Indicates whether communities might feel they are forced to use violent or obstructive behavior as the only way to get company attention
Is the external relations budget determined as a fixed percentage of operational expenditure?	Provides a sense of whether the corporate approach is needs-driven or budget-driven
Are external stakeholder relations in any way reflected in the overall reward structure of all company staff, like safety? If not, is it part of the performance of any staff?	Provides a sense of whether ownership for establishing and maintaining positive community relations exists only within the ERD or is broadly shared among all staff

Figure 13.4 (from previous page)

THE QUESTION	WHAT THE ANSWER TELLS US
Is the engagement approach based on a long-term plan agreed upon with communities and an explicit strategy to achieve this plan?	Provides a sense of the rigor by which external relations are approached or to what extent objectives are systematically linked to the business case
Are external relations in any way integrated into the project design? How? When does the ERD officially know about technical plans or projects?	Indicates whether the external relations staff serve a reactive, or fire-fighting, function or if their knowledge is used to prevent company–community issues from arising
Are incidents and the company response documented and analyzed and, if so, how are the lessons learned fed back into the organization?	Provides a sense of the corporate commitment to addressing community concerns
Who in the organization is accountable for solving tensions with local stakeholders?	Provides a sense of the degree of impunity for making preventable mistakes and of the risks of reoccurrence
Do the same types of community incidents occur repeatedly? Are the basic causes the same or not? Are there SOPs or protocols to address the recurrent issues?	Provides a sense both of the institutional learning capacity of the company and the of the level of standardization within the organization
Does the company take responsibility for stakeholder relations on behalf of contractors? If not, are there contractual provisions for how contractors should deal with communities?	Provides a sense of how seriously management takes the responsibility for getting it right
How does the company measure whether it is successful in its interactions with local communities?	Provides a sense of the degree to which the company is systematic in its approach to stakeholder engagement

14

Measuring the effectiveness of stakeholder engagement

As local stakeholder engagement becomes a more important aspect of corporate operations and the resources allocated to it are increasing, so are management demands to measure the effectiveness of community approaches and returns on community investment.

Companies acknowledge that they do not have effective mechanisms or systems for measuring effectiveness in community relations except when the relationship goes wrong and the company faces threats, demonstrations, or worse. Rather than only knowing that things have gone wrong because a crisis erupts, managers want to find ways to anticipate, and therefore prevent, negative actions.

What is the issue?

Companies frequently find it difficult to measure their effectiveness in achieving positive company–community relations because:

1. **They lack a clear idea of what they want to achieve.** When you do not know what the objective is, it is impossible to define benchmarks for progress toward achieving it.

2. **They do not know how communities define success and whether the company definition matches the community definition.** Clearly, a company can be successful in its community relations only if the community feels it is successful — because community perceptions are the basis for positive or negative company–community relations.

3. **They lack of a baseline to measure changes against.** When there is no clarity about a starting point, there is no basis from which to assess change.

4. **They measure the wrong things.** When a company counts its inputs (number of schools it has built) and outputs (number of students who enroll) but does not assess outcomes (what the students actually learned) and impacts (how schooling changed the students' and their families' and community's well-being), it misses the basic parameters that determine whether communities feel positive or negative toward the company. Further, when companies concentrate on things they can measure quantitatively, they may well overlook the importance of community *perceptions*, which are at the heart of company–community relations.

5. **They assume a direct link of project and program outcomes with overall company objectives.** Companies are often not clear whether or how individual project success relates to an overall company objective such as creating community goodwill for the corporate presence, mitigating social risk, or establishing a long-term positive legacy. It is possible for a company to have some effective individual programs and still experience anger and unhappiness from most surrounding communities. As noted so often in this book, the goodwill generated by a community relations project can be totally undermined by the negative impacts of some operational decision or action.

Getting it right

Define and agree on what success means for the company and for the community

Because success in company–community relations is a shared success, it is imperative that companies consult with communities to arrive at an agreed-to definition of objectives. This is particularly important because CEP sees that many companies have minimal and/or negative definitions of success (disruptions do not happen), whereas communities' hopes are more often positive and combine tangible and intangible factors (such as jobs *and* neighborliness).

Such community consultation could produce a clear set of objectives that satisfy expectations of both company and community. Alternatively, consultation can highlight differences in perspectives that need to be addressed. For example, if a company were to define success in terms of providing improved infrastructure for communities, but communities defined it as improved employment opportunities for youth, it would be important for them to discuss their different emphases. Were they to explore their approaches as partners, they could likely arrive at an agreed-to approach. For example, the company could build roads and clinics but do so in a way that employed a number of youth in the construction process and that provided apprenticeships in construction techniques to improve youths' skills for future employment.

Define and agree on appropriate benchmarks and indicators of success

Company consultation with communities about success also allows them to agree on appropriate benchmarks and indicators for assessing progress (or regression). A company should ask, "How will we know if your perceptions of us are positive or improving (or changing for the worse)? What do you see as our impacts and how do you judge these? Are they beneficial or negative?" Many people in communities will have very concrete and sensible answers that will guide the company in assessing its impacts (beyond inputs, outputs, and outcomes).

Without consultation with communities, companies may make incorrect assumptions about what indicators are showing. For example, a company may interpret a decrease in grievances as an indicator of improving community relations (and decreasing risk to the company). However, in some instances we have seen, a reduction in the number of filed grievances reflects not improved relations but an increasing distrust and cynicism that the company is willing to handle them properly.

Keep in touch with communities to learn of changing goals and expectations

Over the course of a project's phases, people's aspirations may evolve. Their definition of success may be quite high and unrealistic in the early days of a company's construction but, as they get to know and trust company operations, communities may adjust goals to a more realistic — and achievable — level. Or over time, as people become acquainted with the opportunities that the corporate presence provides, their expectations may rise and their definitions of success may shift to higher goals.

Once success and benchmarks are agreed, gather baseline information to gauge change

Baseline information should be focused on what people have said matters to them in their definition of success. For example, if people indicate that they define success as increasing crop outputs, then crop data are important. If their definition has to do with income levels, then baseline earnings should be documented. If success entails trust and respect, then attitude surveys that gather current perceptions of the company are central.

Such a baseline can be a useful tool to remind communities of their early ideas about the presence of the company and the success that they sought as, over time, changes occur. This baseline also helps companies see if and when community definitions of success are changing. If communities have rising expectations that change their success definition, early data collection can at least help them understand how many of their earlier aspirations have, in fact, been achieved.

Use and abuse of indicators

Companies should develop indicators to monitor their progress and achievements with regard to community engagement. Indicators are contextually relevant signals that agreed-to benchmarks are being achieved. Indicators are not goals or final objectives in themselves. Rather, they are *signs* that point to progress, or regression, toward meeting a goal. A reasonable goal for company–community relations might be that people see that the company's presence has improved their lives. Indicators of this will vary in different locations depending on how people define the improvements they hope the company will bring.

Even as companies and communities agree on the definition of success, and the indicators and benchmarks they will monitor to assess progress toward goals, companies should develop systems for monitoring changes in community perceptions about the company. That is, concentrating only on indicators (e.g., how many times do people wave or throw rocks at passing company trucks) may miss true perceptions. It may be correct to interpret waves as indicators of positive perceptions and rocks as indicators of negative perceptions. However, most people may neither wave nor throw rocks so over-interpretation of such signals may be misleading. Therefore, to be sure that the waving/rock-throwing indicator really reflects community perceptions, a company would need to develop a system for assessing broader attitudes to test the accuracy of the specific indicator in reflecting perceptions.

If companies overemphasize indicators detached from the developments they are supposed to reflect, staff may start to manage around achieving indicators rather than goals. For example, in one location, a company used press coverage as an indicator of community relations. When there were no negative stories, they mistakenly believed that relations were good or improving. However, a closer look showed that company staff were making arrangements with journalists to get them to agree not to write any negative stories. Overall community perceptions of the company were negative; a lack of negative press was misleading. If the community also was aware that journalists and company staff were making deals, this could have made people even more mistrustful of the company and its concern for their welfare.

Some important considerations in developing indicators

As noted, the development of key indicators should be context-specific; indicators should always be connected to and reflect company and community objectives. Nonetheless, there are some rules that apply across contexts for effective identification and use of indicators.

Use both quantitative and qualitative indicators

One company hires an independent institution to measure the quantifiable impact of its alternative livelihood program *and*, in addition, also conducts a biannual perception survey to assess attitudes of people toward the company.

Most companies find it easier to identify quantitative indicators than qualitative ones. In part, this is because, as we have noted, many companies define their community relations programs in terms of physical inputs such as clinics built or outputs such as incomes raised. Clearly, to really understand whether clinics or income changes represent success in company–community relations, one needs to find out if people see these as good. Incomes may rise but communities who expected even more benefits may feel the increases were symbolic and insufficient.

So, to assess progress toward real success, companies need to face up to the importance of qualitative indicators. One way to demystify qualitative indicators is to consider how quantitative and qualitative factors interact. For example, to find out if people *feel* more secure as a result of a company's presence (an intangible qualitative factor), one can look at physical, countable factors such as whether parents allow their children to walk to school alone, the normal range of movement of people (in a tight local community or across a broader geographical space), the number of new houses or other personal assets that people are investing in, and the like. Such indicators can point to changes in local perceptions of security, turning a "soft" indicator into a measurable one. Asking people how they feel about security is good; also looking at the objective (measurable) evidence of how they act more or less secure can inform this assessment.

Use both positive and negative indicators

To capture real change, it is important to look at both increases in positive things and decreases in negative things. To highlight only one side of the equation can be misleading and counterproductive. For example, if a company assesses improved community relations in terms of a reduction in threats, this may be misleading if threats have dropped off because the security force has taken draconian measures to punish anyone who threatens the company. Communities would not like the company any more than previously (in fact, they probably would dislike it more); they simply would be quiet about their dislike. Or, using reduced threats as an indicator could be counterproductive. For example, if a company relied on reduction of negative events as its primary community relations indicator, staff could begin to avoid contact with communities in order to avoid anything that might evoke a negative response. Over time, however, increasing distance between company staff and local people would produce less, not more, respect and trust for the company. The signals sent by staff avoiding contact with communities would probably make people dislike the company more, rather than less.

Looking only at positive trends may mask negative factors. For example, a company may monitor incomes and find that its activities have brought prosperity to a community. However, we noted a number of negative impacts that can result when there is a marked influx of cash to areas with little previous cash experience. Increasing wealth for one community may activate jealousy and conflict with neighboring areas where incomes have not risen. Newly wealthy men may exert political power disrupting systems of traditional leadership. The point here is that a company should gather evidence across a spectrum of indicators in order to gain an accurate sense of overall community perceptions and how they are changing.

Use key performance indicators and survey capacities that already exist

Most countries have a government agency responsible for periodic national surveys on health, demographics, education, and so on. Such agencies are often supported by the World Bank or other international institutions that have an interest in acquiring reliable statistics about economic and social trends. Some companies engage such existing agencies to conduct specific surveys in their footprint area. There are several advantages of using such an approach. Indicators that are used by national institutions provide a company with a basis for measuring its impact by comparing results in their area with other parts of the country. In addition, moni-

Table 14.1 **Social performance indicators: company–community relations**
(continued over)

When a company has local support for its approach	When support is compromised (leading indicators)	When a company has no support for its approach (lagging indicators)
• New notices from the company remain on the bulletin boards without being torn off	• Community leaders, elders state they do not feel respected	• Rising trends in theft (no reporting and company is seen as target)
• Evidence that communities are increasingly able to organize themselves due to corporate presence (e.g., through community-based organization, civil society groups, the absence of leadership tussles, etc.)	• The same problems arise over and over	• Work stoppages
	• Evidence that individuals, rather than the community, benefit from company–community interaction	• Increased demands and hostile tone of community
	• Staff feel unsafe visiting communities	• No leniency when accidents happen
• Recognition in the community that the company is bringing opposing groups and parties together that otherwise would not meet	• Cold reception in community during company visits	• Bad press
	• Accusations of company association with a repressive government	• Increasing crime in the area of operations
• Low, or decreasing, theft levels, destruction of company properties	• Disproportional negative reaction compared to the nature of an incident	• Increased conflict between communities or within communities
• The absence, or decreasing trend, of community incidents, or complaints (silence itself is not an indicator)	• Community accusations that the company is "arrogant", not "caring"	• Kidnappings, targeted assaults toward the company
• People associate improvements in their quality of life with the presence of the company	• Visible change in community behavior e.g., people stop greeting (waving to) company staff	• Sabotage
		• Increasing reliance on police/army
• Outsiders campaigning on an anti-corporate platform (journalists, NGOs, politicians) get no local support	• Proliferation of groups that each claim the company should deal with them	• Communities say the company is "stealing" resources
• Community requests are benefiting the community rather than individuals	• Communities demand that company benefits need to be negotiated (e.g., via memoranda of understanding)	
• Community requests focus on personal skills development instead of demand for material things	• Groups of people hanging around at the company gates hoping to get work	
• No or low public outrage		

Table 14.1 (from previous page)

When a company has local support for its approach	When support is compromised (leading indicators)	When a company has no support for its approach (lagging indicators)
• Communities identify trouble-makers and inform company staff about (security) rumors in the community		
• Communities say they have access to corporate decision makers and say the company is responsive to their concerns		
• People wave back when greeted		
• Continuously high attendance rates for meetings when no seating allowance is being paid		

toring and evaluation efforts that are strategically linked with ongoing efforts may be more cost-effective and sustainable because government will continue such surveys after a company leaves. Using a government agency, rather than a contractor hired by the company, can also increase the credibility of the survey outcomes.

Although there is no single indicator that is always the most relevant across all contexts, there are many ways of knowing whether things are going better or worse in community relations (see Tables 14.1, 14.2, and 14.3). It is not difficult to maintain broad company awareness of these indicators and, over time, to discover which are most useful and important in any given context. Managers who are themselves attentive to these signals, and who support their staff in awareness and reporting of shifts in them, will find they are able to avoid extreme negative reactions of communities. They will enjoy increasingly positive company–community relations.

Table 14.2 **Social performance indicators: company–government relations**

When a company has local support for its approach	When support is compromised (leading indicators)	When a company has no support for its approach (lagging indicators)
• Government officials state the company keeps them informed • The government increases its social services presence in the corporate area • Government officials are present and are responsive to company as well as to community requests • The government states the corporate presence has allowed them to be more effective • Government officials (civil servants) say they feel more legitimized/ respected in the community due to the corporate presence • The government discusses with the company: upcoming regulations, etc.	• Government presence in the area of operation is primarily through the military • Government expects company to build community infrastructure • Government disengages from the area of corporate operations • Reliance on bribery to get the government to fulfil its duties • Limited access of company staff to government officials • Government interference with internal company policies (e.g., staff hiring/lay-off) • Both government and company state that the other party is responsible for community relations	• Government encourages communities to demand (and expect) provision of social services from the company • State security forces are involved in sabotage activities against the company • State security forces are a risk to corporate staff and assets • Security forces associated with the company commit human rights abuses • Government revenues are explicitly used for warfare or violence against the citizenry

Table 14.3 **Social performance indicators: company–critics relations**

When a company has local support for its approach	When support is compromised (leading indicators)	When a company has no support for its approach (lagging indicators)
• Journalists highlight the benefits of a corporate presence • Credible NGOs wish to be associated with the company • No local presence of advocacy NGOs • The company's practices are regarded as among the best by outside groups	• Questions are raised regarding company actions from home government • International advocacy NGOs critical of company actions start establishing local branches • Company is mentioned on activist websites (getting on their radar screen) • Company accused of having an arrogant, defensive or legalistic tone • Refusal of NGOs to meet with the company	• NGOs encourage community demonstrations against the company • NGO advocacy campaigns against company • Divestment campaign/ consumer boycotts • Shareholder activism critical of company actions • Websites against the company • NGOs and lawyers actively seeking witnesses for court cases • Litigation

15

'Even engineers can get it right . . .'

Some years ago, a CEP team was having lunch in the canteen at the field site of a major oil company and, as we ate, struck up a conversation with an engineering consultant who was also on-site for a few days. In the course of the conversation, the consultant asked what CEP was all about.

We explained that our concern was with ensuring that companies' activities made communities better off, rather than worse off, and that our process involved many site visits to different companies in different settings to determine the patterns by which positive and negative impacts occur. As we described what we were learning, the consultant began to laugh. "You think just like an engineer," he said.

> " Engineers work with flow-through processes. They examine how if 'x' goes in one end, and moves through the 'pipeline' of the engineering process, but the 'y' that comes out is not what was expected, then the engineers go back and examine every part of the pipeline to determine where, in the process, something happened to create the unexpected outcome. This is exactly what you are doing too! "

We, the CEP team, were struck by the analogy. This consultant was exactly right. As we noted in the opening chapter of this book, when companies locate in remote areas, both the company management and the community where they locate want, and expect, that their relations will be cordial, cooperative, and productive. No one *sets out* to get it wrong.

Yet, over time, as the result of many seemingly disconnected decisions or actions, company–community relations deteriorate and, too often, become impediments to smooth production. Managers start out expecting a certain "y" to emerge at the end of their interactions with communities and are surprised when difficulties emerge.

But CEP finds that, at the point when company–community relations start to deteriorate, many managers throw their hands up in dismay, saying that they "simply cannot understand those people." At this point, well-trained engineers give up the analytic process in which they are trained that would help them understand and, instead, conclude that they are powerless to solve the problems they encounter.

In such settings, CEP often hears people, including engineers themselves, speak about the "engineering mentality." Many claim that people with this mentality are "not programmed" to relate to or to grasp community issues. The explanation becomes an excuse. Some people seem to imply that there is an intrinsic and inevitable engineering approach that cannot be expected to handle company–community relations adeptly.

We do not agree! The evidence is strong that "even engineers" (not *our* language, but quoted from many engineering colleagues) can be "good neighbors" — in the words of local communities. Many with whom we have interacted during the years of CEP's fieldwork have exhibited their basic commitment to positive interactions with local people, and many have shown creativity and imagination in finding workable solutions to seemingly intractable company–community problems.

The discussions in the previous chapters of this book are intended to help "even engineers" learn from their own past and vast experience. They are intended to help engineers, managers, and other company personnel apply the same analytic rigor to their investigations of surprising outcomes from company–community interactions as they would apply to solving problems that emerge in a pumping station or a gas pipeline.

All the evidence — and the reader now knows there is quite a lot! — leads to the conclusion that establishing, or improving, relations with communities is very much a practical, step-by-step process that is within the reach of any company and within the reach of any and all staff members of a company.

To take on these lessons, what might a manager do?

If the company is in the process of establishing itself, a manager may review all of the corporate operations that have impacts on communities (and, as is surely clear to the readers of this book, *not* only its community development or community relations approach). A manager could ensure that these operations all reflect and fit local definitions of fairness, transparency, respect, and broad accountability. As a matter of rigor, making the most prevalent corporate assumptions explicit *and testing the validity of these* with local staff, advisors, or other local actors would be a relatively straightforward exercise and not dissimilar from the flow-through process that engineers use in many other aspects of their operations.

For existing operations, a manager might take a clear inventory of where things now stand with communities. Are there shutdowns and strikes? Complaints?

Threats? From whom? How often? Does the company receive positive feedback? Does it have a system in place to track positive signals? How? Recognizing the reality of what one is working with is, of course, essential to addressing real issues. Or a manager might review all the systems that are in place for benefits distribution and analyze how transparent they are, how they may favor some groups over others, whether they feed into and promote dividers or connectors, or reward violence or encourage reasonableness and, with this clarity, make appropriate changes in these systems. Or a manager might issue a series of directives to staff specifying the SOPs for behavior on and off the job that show respect to local culture. All of these are aspects of a useful process.

The first step toward positive company–community relations

However, if the CEP staff who have spent these years working with managers around the world were able to recommend one specific action for any manager, anywhere, to take first, it would be the following.

Ask a local person whom you trust and who is respected by other local people to take you to the communities that are affected by your operations. This could be someone you have hired locally — a driver or an engineer, a security guard or a community relations officer. But you should be sure that the person has an easy, comfortable relationship with other people in the communities where you will visit.

When this person takes you to communities (multiple communities, over a period of several days), get out of your car and walk around and talk with people. Ask them how they are. Listen to them. Be relaxed and willing to sit down and talk. In your conversations, ask specifically, "What are the impacts on your life of the company's being here? What are the pluses, the positive impacts for you? What are the downsides, the negative impacts that concern you? And, what do you suggest we do to make sure that we sustain the positives and begin to address some of these negatives?"

A manager who is seen to be asking these questions with a broad range of people (not just a few) in full view of others (so the conversations are transparent) and listening (really listening) to the responses of all these people would accomplish two immediate benefits.

First, this process would send important messages that the management is not afraid and distrustful of local people, that they want to hear and learn from local ideas and that they respect the holders of these ideas, and that they want to be accountable for direct and indirect company impacts. These messages are important for the establishment of a healthy relationship.

Second, the manager will probably hear some very important concerns and some surprisingly positive ideas that could prove to be the keys for untangling complicated company–community interactions. Many local people *do* have ideas and many of these contain elements of solutions to problems that may not be imagined from inside the manager's office. Locally grounded solutions are what a good manager looks for. One source for such ideas must be people who live their lives in the context where problems arise.

As the preceding chapters have shown, there are many layers and aspects of negative — or positive — company–community relations. It behooves a company to require that its managers recognize and work with these in all their complex interactions. It is never appropriate to over-simplify the challenges that face complex societies undergoing extraordinary change and the challenges that these pose for those that work within such societies.

At the same time, some immediate, doable, and simple steps can pay back in extraordinary benefits as the first steps for establishing positive relations or for moving toward solutions to the multi-layered problems companies encounter with communities. Many of these are suggested in the pages of this book. Managers who look for alternative ways of operating will, we feel sure based on our CEP experience, continue to find as-yet-unknown, productive options. Building on what has been learned from experience provides a strong base for much more learning. Companies and communities have started on a road together that has many more miles ahead. Each needs to find ways to travel this road that improves the lives and livelihoods of people along the way.

About the authors

Mary B. Anderson is the Executive Director of CDA Collaborative Learning Projects. Mary earned her PhD in Economics from the University of Colorado in Boulder and held a post-doctorate appointment at the Massachusetts Institute of Technology. She has served as Program Associate for the Harvard Institute for International Development and as Acting Director of the Bunting Institute at Radcliffe College. Her international work began in 1961 in East Africa where she worked as a Community Development Assistant for the Tanganyikan (now Tanzanian) government, living in villages in the Northern and Central Provinces. Since then, she has worked in over 70 countries in the fields of education, local technology development, conflict analysis and peace building, humanitarianism, and development. She has consulted with governments, the World Bank, United Nations agencies and numerous non-governmental NGOs. She is the author of numerous articles, programming documents, and of several books that deal with humanitarian and development assistance in poor or warring societies. She has been closely engaged in the work that produced this book, involved in several of the site visits and headquarters consultations from which the lessons were derived.

Luc Zandvliet is the Director of the Corporate Engagement Project at CDA Collaborative Learning Projects. He earned an MSc in Personnel Management at Tilburg University in the Netherlands and an MA in Humanitarian Assistance at The Fletcher School of Law and Diplomacy at Tufts University. He has worked with humanitarian agencies such as Médecins Sans Frontières–Holland and the International Committee of the Red Cross in various crisis areas, often the same areas where companies also have a presence. These experiences prompted him to ask how it is possible to make sure that corporations have positive, rather than negative, impacts on the lives of local stakeholders. This book is the result of that query. Since the Corporate Engagement Project began in 2000, Luc visited over 25 company sites in 16 countries in his work with CDA and he was involved in the majority of the fieldwork conducted for this book. He is currently working on integrating the lessons learned through the Corporate Engagement Project in new applications such as human rights risk assessments, risk assessment tools for the financial industry, and training and coaching approaches for field-based company staff.

Index